WITHDRAWAL

Kim Jong Il

Other books in the People in the News series:

Al Gore
David Beckham
Beyoncé
Fidel Castro
Kelly Clarkson
Hillary Clinton
Hilary Duff
Dale Earnhardt Jr.
Zac Efron
50 Cent
Al Gore
Tony Hawk
Salma Hayek
LeBron James
Angelina Jolie
Ashton Kutcher
Tobey Maguire
John McCain
Barack Obama
Nancy Pelosi
Queen Latifah
Condoleezza Rice
J.K. Rowling
Shakira
Tupac Shakur
Ben Stiller
Hilary Swank
Justin Timberlake
Usher

Kim Jong Il

by Sheila Wyborny

LUCENT BOOKS
A part of Gale, Cengage Learning

 GALE
CENGAGE Learning™

Detroit • New York • San Francisco • New Haven, Conn • Waterville, Maine • London

GALE
CENGAGE Learning™

LIBRARY OF CONGRESS CATALOGING-IN-PUBLICATION DATA

Wyborny, Sheila, 1950-
  Kim Jong Il / by Sheila Wyborny.
    p. cm. -- (People in the news)
  Includes bibliographical references and index.
  ISBN 978-1-4205-0091-2 (hardcover)
  1. Kim, Chong-il, 1942—Juvenile literature. 2. Heads of state--Korea (North)--Biography--Juvenile literature. 3. Korea (North—Politics and government--Juvenile literature. I. Title.
  DS934.6.K44W93 2009
  951.9305'1092—dc22
  [B]
                                                    2008049567

Lucent Books
27500 Drake Rd
Farmington Hills MI 48331

ISBN-13: 978-1-4205-0091-2
ISBN-10: 1-4205-0091-0

Contents

F ame and celebrity are alluring. People are drawn to those who walk in fame's spotlight, whether they are known for great accomplishments or for notorious deeds. The lives of the famous pique public interest and attract attention, perhaps because their experiences seem in some ways so different from, yet in other ways so similar to, our own.

Newspapers, magazines, and television regularly capitalize on this fascination with celebrity by running profiles of famous people. For example, television programs such as *Entertainment Tonight* devote all of their programming to stories about entertainment and entertainers. Magazines such as *People* fill their pages with stories of the private lives of famous people. Even newspapers, newsmagazines, and television news frequently delve into the lives of well-known personalities. Despite the number of articles and programs, few provide more than a superficial glimpse at their subjects.

Lucent's People in the News series offers young readers a deeper look into the lives of today's newsmakers, the influences that have shaped them, and the impact they have had in their fields of endeavor and on other people's lives. The subjects of the series hail from many disciplines and walks of life. They include authors, musicians, athletes, political leaders, entertainers, entrepreneurs, and others who have made a mark on modern life and who, in many cases, will continue to do so for years to come.

These biographies are more than factual chronicles. Each book emphasizes the contributions, accomplishments, or deeds that have brought fame or notoriety to the individual and shows how that person has influenced modern life. Authors portray their subjects in a realistic, unsentimental light. For example, Bill Gates—the cofounder and chief executive officer of the software giant Microsoft—has been instrumental in making personal computers the most vital tool of the modern age. Few dispute his business savvy, his perseverance, or his technical expertise, yet critics say he is ruthless in his dealings with competitors and driven more by his desire to maintain Microsoft's dominance in the computer industry than by an interest in furthering technology.

In these books, young readers will encounter inspiring stories about real people who achieved success despite enormous obstacles. Oprah Winfrey—the most powerful, most watched, and wealthiest woman on television today—spent the first six years of her life in the care of her grandparents while her unwed mother sought work and a better life elsewhere. Her adolescence was colored by promiscuity, pregnancy at age fourteen, rape, and sexual abuse.

Each author documents and supports his or her work with an array of primary and secondary source quotations taken from diaries, letters, speeches, and interviews. All quotes are footnoted to show readers exactly how and where biographers derive their information and provide guidance for further research. The quotations enliven the text by giving readers eyewitness views of the life and accomplishments of each person covered in the People in the News series.

In addition, each book in the series includes photographs, annotated bibliographies, timelines, and comprehensive indexes. For both the casual reader and the student researcher, the People in the News series offers insight into the lives of today's newsmakers—people who shape the way we live, work, and play in the modern age.

Controversy and Contradictions

Putting together a profile of North Korean leader Kim Jong Il is like trying to assemble a particularly difficult jigsaw puzzle. It is hard to make all of the pieces fit properly. Information about him depends upon the source. For example, in the biography posted on the official homepage of the Democratic People's Republic of Korea, Kim Jong Il receives glowing praise: "Sharing joy and sorrow with the people at all times and through genuine popular politics, the benevolent politics, he has made the whole country a large revolutionary family in which all people are united around the party and the leader. He has also shown deep concern to providing the Korean people with worthwhile and happy lives."[1]

At the other end of the spectrum, though, people view him in a far less flattering light: "Systematic human rights abuses throughout North Korea have been rampant and well-documented during Kim's reign. It is estimated that there are some 200,000 political prisoners in the country today; there have been innumerable reports of torture, slave labor, and forced abortions and infanticides in the prison camps."[2]

Dear Leader or Devil in Disguise?

The truth about Kim Jong Il, what kind of a person he is and what kind of a leader he is, probably lies somewhere between these two

Controversial North Korean leader Kim Jong Il assumed control in 1994 after the death of his father, Kim Il Sung, building his country's military despite its severe economic and social hardships and international criticism.

observations. What is known from fairly reliable sources is that he is a small man, probably a couple of inches over five feet, and, in addition to sporting a pompadour, a poufy hairstyle popular in the 1950s which adds a bit to his height, it is rumored he wears lifts in his shoes to add to the appearance of height as well.

South Korean intelligence sources have stated at various times that he is a madman, a heavy drinker, and a womanizer. However, they have also credited him with a genius IQ, and some say he is an expert with computers. Additionally, he has been accused by some sources of ordering two bombings, both prior to taking leadership of the country. The first was in 1983 in what was then Rangoon, Burma, in which seventeen visiting South Korean officials were killed. The other was in 1987 onboard a South Korean airliner. This explosion claimed the lives of all 115 passengers.

However, North Korean publications often refer to Kim as "Dear Leader," and there is little doubt he is a skilled strategist. When his father, the former North Korean leader, Kim Il Sung, died suddenly from a heart attack in 1994 at age 82, many political experts believed the country would fall apart. Its alliances with China as well as the Soviet bloc had already disintegrated, and the economy was essentially destroyed. Additionally, climate problems, such as severe drought, and an inefficiently run state-controlled agricultural system drained the food supply.

These were the conditions in the country when Kim Jong Il inherited leadership from his father. For a while, Kim disappeared from the public eye, but he used this time very productively. He totally reorganized the political structure of North Korea and built his military resources until he had the fourth largest military structure in the world. This fact is all the more impressive, considering the size of North Korea, which is roughly comparable in size to the states of Mississippi or Alabama.

Nuclear Capabilities: Bargaining Chip or Blackmail?

However, his military is not all Kim Jong Il has been building over the years in North Korea. The country began building a nuclear arsenal while Kim's father was in power. The extent of North Korean nuclear weaponry is an issue surrounded by mystery and suspicion. No one is certain exactly what weapons and technology North Korea has in their possession. It is a fact, though, that North Korea has been developing missile technology and did, indeed, launch a medium-range, multi-stage rocket over Japan in 1998. Additionally, under Kim's father's direction, though some experts attribute it to Kim himself, North Korea supplied hotspots in the Middle East, such as Iran and Pakistan, with this deadly technology. This behavior flagrantly violated the 1994 Framework Agreement with the United States, an agreement whereby North Korea agreed to stop producing nuclear weapons. Because of this, the United States and some allies imposed economic sanctions against North Korea.

This did not stop Kim. North Korean officials said that if the United States wanted North Korea to stop the missile exports, the United States must lift the sanctions and compensate the North Koreans for the income they would lose if they stopped selling their nuclear technology to the Middle East. Even though the United States lifted the sanctions in 1999, Kim continued his deadly exports. After more years of failed negotiations, the United States and its allies cut fuel shipments that had been promised to North Korea in 2002. Since then Kim and his country have continued developing nuclear technology, while promising this development is for peaceful purposes, yet threatening war if the United States or its allies make strikes on North Korean nuclear facilities.

These developments of the last decade show no signs of coming to an end. To date, Kim Jong Il continues to develop his nuclear weapons program, ignoring international agreements. Whether a madman or brilliant strategist, Kim, leader of a country about the size of a small American state, flaunts North Korean nuclear power and threatens retaliation should any country or countries call his hand.

Chapter 1

Privilege and Power

To better understand the behavior of Kim Jong Il, it is first necessary to know something of the political climate of the region and the times in which Kim was born and raised, and also how the life experiences of his parents may have influenced him. It is also important to understand some of the events he may have witnessed as a child that most likely had an effect on the adult he would become.

For most of the first half of the twentieth century, Korea was under the control of a foreign power, Japan. In 1904 Japan and Russia fought a war over control of Korea. Japan won. At that time, Japan was a far different type of country than the modern, technologically advanced country it is today. In fact, some of the ways Japan dealt with other countries and the people of those countries were quite vicious. The time Korea spent under Japanese control was a period of brutal domination and cruelty. Because of this, the Koreans resented and feared the Japanese, especially the Japanese secret police. The Japanese were seen as invaders. They often dealt harshly with the Korean people, imprisoning, assaulting, and sometimes killing anyone who defied them.

In an effort to overthrow the Japanese and regain their freedom, the Koreans formed guerrilla fighting groups and other resistance units. Since the Japanese occupied Korea for nearly forty years, sometimes two or even three generations within the same family became resistance workers or guerrilla fighters. Kim Jong Il's family was a part of the resistance movement. Kim's own

Entrenched Japanese troops battle during their 1904–1905 war against Russia over control of Korea, which was occupied by Japan for nearly forty years, until its defeat by Allied forces in World War II.

grandfather had fought for the resistance and died after a period of imprisonment. Long before Kim's birth, his father and also his mother were resistance fighters.

Family Background

According to some sources, Kim Jong Il's father, Kim Il Sung, was born Kim Song Juh, the son of converted Christians. These same reports state that he changed his name to that of a respected resistance leader. Regardless of the name he had at birth, though, according to most sources, Kim Il Sung was born in April 1912 in the village of Mangyong-dae, near Pyongyang, Korea, the eldest of three sons. The family had lived in the village since Kim Il Sung's great-grandfather's time. Both his father and grandfather had been farmers, and his father also sold herbal medicines.

Farming is not an easy way of life, but it was especially hard for this family. Korea had fallen under Japanese rule in 1910, two years prior to Kim Il Sung's birth. Times were so hard for his family that there were days the family was reduced to eating grain meant for cattle feed, because their crops had been taken by the Japanese. "I still recall how much trouble I had swallowing those coarse hard-to-digest grains,"[3] he later remarked.

Uniformed Japanese soldiers pose among Korean villagers in 1910. Many Koreans resented Japan's harsh rule over their nation and thus joined the resistance movement to overthrow their occupiers.

When Kim Il Sung was a small child, his father left home during the winter months, joining Chinese guerrilla fighters to fight the Japanese, who were trying to take over their countries and wipe out their cultures. He was one of many Koreans who wanted to overthrow the Japanese. Not only did these invaders control their country, they changed nearly everything about Korean culture and enslaved its people. An elite class of scholars, military officers, and government officials had once ruled the country. When Japan took over, they placed the country under the control of a resident-general. The Japanese coerced the Koreans to build factories and roads, took the food grown by the farmers, and forced many farmers off land they had occupied and worked for generations. They even replaced the national language with Japanese and insisted the Koreans practice Shinto, the religion of Japan. Basically, the Japanese did everything they could to wipe out the culture and traditions of Korea.

The Korean people rebelled, though. In March 1919, when Kim Il Sung was about seven years old, the people of his village and other villages, including schoolchildren, staged a large protest called the March First Movement. They marched to the gates of the Pyongyang Castle, where the Japanese officials lived. Japanese soldiers attacked the villagers and children. Many Koreans were injured or killed during the march. Others who participated were later tortured and killed. Kim Il Sung's father had already been jailed once for his part in resistance activities. Supposedly, young Kim Il Sung was one of the child marchers. If so, he witnessed this brutality. Such events would have a deep and lasting effect on a child.

Finally, conditions became so bad in the village that, when Kim Il Sung was eight years old, his father moved his family 250 miles (402.34 km) from their home to Joong-gang, a town in rough mountainous terrain, near the northern border of Korea. His father soon discovered that his name was on a blacklist (a list of suspicious persons to be watched and/or penalized) even this far from the capital, so he moved his family even farther, into the part of China known as Manchuria. There, the family operated an herbal shop. Young Kim was sent to school to learn the language of the country. At first, he resented this, but later he was glad that he had learned the language.

A teenaged Kim Il Sung, reared by resistance-fighter parents, joined the Communist Party as part of his efforts to combat Japan's control of Korea, a decision that got him expelled from school and arrested.

When Kim was about twelve years old, his father was again arrested for his work with the resistance forces. He later escaped, but suffered severe frostbite. Due to his weakened condition from imprisonment and the hardships of his escape, Kim's father became severely ill. Supposedly, on his deathbed, he gave Kim his pistol and begged him to join the fight against the Japanese.

He died in June 1926. Fourteen-year-old Kim Il Sung blamed the Japanese for his father's death and grew to hate them even more. The next year, he joined the Communist Party, who actively resisted Japanese domination. This caused him to be expelled from school, and some time later, he was briefly arrested for his involvement with the party. When Japan attacked China in 1931, the Chinese and the exiled Koreans united in their efforts to fight the Japanese. Kim Il Sung became a guerrilla fighter.

During Kim Il Sung's time as a guerrilla fighter, he met Kim Jung Suk, who, herself, had been active in the guerrilla movement for half a dozen years. They were stationed at the same guerrilla camp in Siberia. Like Kim Il Sung, Kim Jung Suk was from a family of poor farmers. Also like his family, after persecution by the Japanese, her family fled Korea to live in China, where as a five-year-old child she worked in the fields alongside her family. They earned their living as sharecroppers, raising crops for the property owner in return for a portion of those crops. The property owner took her older sister and forced her to work as his servant because her parents could not repay a debt they owed him.

Mount Paektu

At 9,022 feet (2750 meters), Mt. Paektu, the fabled birthplace of Kim Jong Il, is the highest mountain peak in Korea. A log cabin, Kim's alleged birthplace, lies near Jong Il Peak, a cliff outcropping in the forest. The cabin is a popular Korean tourist attraction with its carefully preserved furnishings, including a desk and a lamp, binoculars, and a wooden pistol, said to have belonged to members of Kim's family. Northern Yanggang Province, where the mountain is located, is a place of scenic beauty. It is also the site of the Korean creation legend. According to the legend, Hwanung, a son of the Lord of Heaven, was allowed to descend to Mount Paektu with three thousand followers to found an earthly city on this site.

Another similarity to Kim Il Sung's childhood was that Kim Jung Suk's father died when she was quite young. In 1932, when she was just fifteen years old, two things happened. Her mother and sister-in-law were killed when the Japanese attacked the village where they were living, and she joined the Young Communist League of Korea, a paramilitary organization for children and young people. One of her duties was to distribute leaflets and take part in activities designed to disrupt Japanese activities and businesses. She became the leader of the Children's Corps. Together, corps members collected ammunition for the guerrillas and acted as scouts for them. She also organized a performing troupe, children who performed revolutionary songs and skits. She became a guerrilla fighter in 1934. Two years later, in 1936, she was assigned to a unit under the command of Kim Il Sung. A delicately pretty young woman, she hardly looked like someone who could carry, let alone shoot, a heavy military weapon. In fact, women guerrillas fought alongside the men and were considered their equals. She and Kim were married in 1941, and their first child, a son, was born in 1942.

Early Childhood

There are two accounts of Kim Jong Il's birth. According to one fanciful version, likely generated by the Korean propaganda mill, he was born on the sacred mountain, Mount Paektu, the highest peak on the Korean peninsula. Supposedly, at the time of his birth, lightning bolts flashed through the skies, and the iceberg in the pond on the sacred mountain made a mysterious sound, broke apart, and a double rainbow rose from it. In the more practical account of his birth, Kim Jong Il was born in a guerrilla military camp in the far eastern region of the Soviet Union. His official birth date is given as February 16, 1942.

In what was probably one of his first official photographs, a chubby baby Kim Jong Il, wearing a tiny military uniform with a jauntily tipped cap, salutes the camera as his father laughs indulgently and his mother looks at the camera with a solemn expression. Despite what otherwise appears to be a portrait of an

Toddler Kim Jong Il offers a salute in the company of his parents, Kim Il Sung and Kim Jung Suk, both experienced guerilla fighters dedicated to ending Japan's dominance of Korea and its people.

average young Korean family at one moment in time, this young family was anything but ordinary. Both parents were experienced guerrilla fighters. They were dedicated to wrenching Korea from the control of the Japanese invaders and returning it to the hands of Koreans. If necessary, they were prepared to sacrifice their own lives for that cause.

Kim Jong Il has his own Korean name, but at one time he also had a Russian name. His Russian name was Yuri Irsenovich Kim, and his nickname was Yura. He kept this nickname until he was in his teens. There is not a great deal of information about Kim Jong Il's earliest years in the encampment, but some facts are fairly apparent. For instance, although his parents were very important members of the resistance movement, living conditions in a military camp in one of the coldest regions of the Soviet Union were probably uncomfortable. Also, even as a small child, Kim Jong Il as well as the other children in the encampment were probably taught the beliefs associated with communism, the political philosophy of the guerrillas and the political party that ultimately gained control of the Soviet Union.

In 1945, though, when Kim Jong Il was about three years old, his family had reason to celebrate. After taking two direct hits from atomic bombs dropped by American bomber planes in August of that year, first on Hiroshima, then on Nagasaki, the Japanese made an unconditional surrender. This not only ended their role in World War II but also their domination of Korea.

Korea was not a unified nation, however. It was divided at the thirty-eighth parallel into North Korea, also known as the Democratic People's Republic of Korea, and South Korea. Each portion was occupied by a liberating army, the Soviet Union in the north and American troops in the south. The Soviets placed Kim Jong Il's father in charge of the government of North Korea. Kim Il Sung returned to Korea in September 1945. Kim Jong Il, his mother, and his younger brother, Shura, born in 1944, followed in November. A short time later, baby sister, Kim Kyung Hee, was born. Here, in the capital city of Pyongyang, their living conditions improved drastically.

Due to his father's position, Kim Jong Il's family was part of the privileged class. They had the best food, clothing, and everything else available in Korea. In fact, they moved into a former Japanese officer's mansion. The mansion had a garden and a pool. Their lives were not without tragedy, however. When Kim Jong Il's younger brother was about four years old, he drowned in the pool. Accounts differ regarding this tragedy. According to some, the child died alone in a swimming accident. According to others, though, he died as a result of horseplay in the pool with his older brother. Whatever the cause of the child's death, it was a sad time for Kim Jong Il's family.

Sources even disagree about Kim Jong Il's early education. Some claim he spent his earliest school days in China. According to his official biography, however, Kim Jong Il attended Primary School

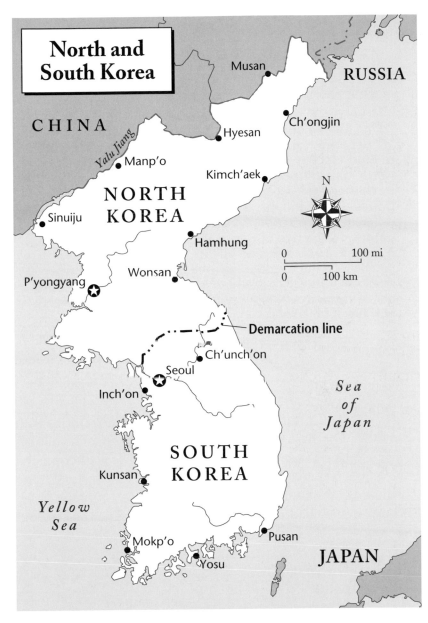

North and South Korea

Musan

RUSSIA

CHINA

Ch'ongjin

Hyesan

Yalu Jiang

Manp'o

Kimch'aek

NORTH
KOREA

Sinuiju

Hamhung

N

Wonsan

0   100 mi

0   100 km

P'yongyang

Demarcation line

Ch'unch'on

Seoul

Inch'on

*Sea
of
Japan*

SOUTH
KOREA

Kunsan

*Yellow
Sea*

Mokp'o

Pusan

JAPAN

Yosu

*The end of World War II saw the Korean peninsula divided
into two nations along the 38th parallel: the Democratic
People's Republic of Korea in the north, under the Soviet-
influenced rule of Kim Il Sung, and the U.S.-supported
Republic of Korea in the south.*

The Korean Conflict

The Korean Conflict began as a result of border clashes between North and South Korea. South Korea refused to hold elections according to North Korean demands. North Korean troops attacked the south on June 25, 1950. Hostilities soon escalated due to the involvement of the United States and the Soviet Union. The hostilities were called a "police action," rather than a war, in an effort to avoid a declaration of war by the United States Congress. A cease fire was called on July 27, 1953. The thirty-eighth parallel and the surrounding area was declared a demilitarized zone. Due to conflicting information, the exact number of casualties from all participating parties combined may never be known.

Number 4, and later Middle School Number 1, in Pyongyang.

All of his education did not take place in the classroom, though. As a young child, Kim Jong Il visited farms and factories with his mother. On these visits, he saw children his age and younger engaged in hard labor alongside their parents. His mother wanted him to understand that with privilege comes responsibility, and that many children in his country were not as fortunate as he. Kim apparently had a close relationship with his mother, but that, too, was cut short. In 1949 his beautiful, but strict, mother died. According to some sources, she died of tuberculosis. Other accounts state that she died in childbirth and that the baby, a girl, did not live either.

What followed was probably a lonely and confusing time for seven-year-old Kim Jong Il and his four-year-old sister. Their mother and brother were dead, and their father was too preoccupied with the government of North Korea to have much time to spend with them. As if this were not enough trouble for two young children to endure, in 1950, their country was once again at war.

The Korean War, also referred to as the Korean Conflict, continued from 1950 to 1953. According to some records, during these years, Kim Jong Il's father sent him and his sister to China, for their safety. While in China, they attended the Mangyong-dae School for Children of Revolutionaries, a school organized for the children of Kim Il Sung's comrades from his anti-Japanese guerrilla fighter days. In addition to the normal subjects children learn in school, Kim Jong Il and his sister, as well as the other children in the school, probably spent many hours each week learning the fundamentals of communism, the social philosophy of China as well as the Soviet Union. This had a strong influence on their political beliefs as adults.

This period of time away from their family and their home country had another effect on them as well. Possibly because they spent this time in exile as virtual orphans and had only each other for comfort during those years, Kim Jong Il and his sister, Kim Kyung Hee, became very devoted to one another. Their close relationship continued into adulthood. She is, in fact, sometimes known as Kim Jong Il's first lady, and it is said he expects her to be treated with the same degree of respect his people show him.

Continuing Education and Early Interests

When the war ended in 1953, their father decided Korea was safe enough for his children and permitted Kim Jong Il, now eleven, and his sister to return. As Kim entered his teen years, he took an active role in student politics. He belonged to the Children's Union and Democratic Youth League (DYL). Like his father, Kim supported the philosophies of communism. Ideally, communism means that land and goods are owned collectively and shared equally by all the people. In reality, though, the government owns the property, and all political, economic, and social activity are controlled by a single political party. Because of his parents' beliefs as well as what he had been taught in school, Kim thought this was the way a country should be run.

As an adolescent, Kim Jong Il eagerly embraced the communist philosophies taught by his parents and at school, resulting in his active interest and involvement in student politics.

According to his official biography, the teenaged Kim was a natural leader, active in most of the communist-sponsored Korean youth organizations and activities. Other accounts, though, describe him differently. Some say he was shy and introverted. Still others say he sometimes acted out and behaved disruptively, even to the point of engaging in risky behavior, although nothing specific is mentioned. He has been described as a bully and disrespectful, and it has been said that he threatened classmates and friends when he was angry with them. In fact, his disrespect toward older people and his superiors is fairly well known, as mentioned in one account. "The traits most frequently mentioned … are Kim's independence, arrogance, and lack of respect for seniors… "[4]

Kim Jong Il attended Namsan Senior High School, a school for the children of the elite, and frequently rode to and from school on his motorcycle. Although he was the son of the most powerful political figure in North Korea, Kim, like other young people his age, did have some interests outside of politics. For instance, he liked automobiles and was interested in the workings of just about any engine. In school workshops, he repaired electric motors and truck engines. In addition to automobiles and engine repair, he maintained his interest in the farms of his country, an interest that carried over from visiting farms with his mother when he was a young child. He also went on tours of factories with his classmates. Finally, like young people throughout the world, Kim was interested in movies and music, two interests that continued throughout his life. Some reports indicate this interest is somewhat obsessive.

Despite any behavioral problems, though, some of which can be attributed to the many ways any child can find to get into trouble, some people remember other qualities from those early days, especially his attention to his father and to political issues in his country. One of the people who knew Kim very well when he was a high school student was Hwang Jang Yop, a one-time top aide to Kim Il Sung. Hwang defected from North Korea in the late 1990s. He said of the young man: "Kim Jong Il was intelligent and full of curiosity, asking me many questions. Despite his young age, he already harbored political ambitions. He paid special attention to his father… Every morning he would help his father to get up and put on his shoes."[5]

While he was still a senior in high school, Kim studied and observed the ways his father attended to the government of North Korea. To win his father's approval, young Kim sometimes sat in on government meetings. Apparently, he tried to do everything he could to stay in his father's good graces. For instance, after graduating from Namsan High School, he traveled to East Germany, where he entered the Air Academy, a pilot's training college. Although the actual period of time he was in the academy is disputed, this supposedly happened at the end of 1959 and the early months of 1960. There is little to indicate whether or not he succeeded in learning to fly an airplane. However, there are numerous reports that Kim Jong Il does not like to fly and is, in fact, terrified of flying. This being the case, it was probably at the urging of his father, or to please his father, that he went to pilots' school. Whether he earned his pilot's wings or not, he left the Air Academy in 1962 and returned to North Korea to complete his college education.

Two Sides of Kim

Many changes took place in Kim Jong Il's life from the time he was born until he became a young man. The greatest change occurred when his father rose from guerrilla warrior in exile to leader of the Democratic People's Republic of Korea. For Kim, whose early childhood was spent in military encampments, his life became one of vast wealth and many privileges. Despite the glowing praise heaped on the young man by state-controlled media, the way Kim Jong Il actually lived and conducted himself might not have been as inspirational as portrayed. For example, with his lavish lifestyle, he could have whatever type of car he wanted and any kind of food he preferred, regardless of cost. Additionally, servants, government employees, and even the professors at the university went out of their way to attend to his every need and fulfill his every wish.

From University to Graduation

According to official records, Kim Jong Il entered the Political/ Economic Department of the College of Economics at Kim Il Sung University in September 1960. According to these same records, the accounts provided by the state-run television, press, and official government press releases, Kim was a busy and dedicated

Kim Il Sung, right, poses with students at the university bearing his name in 1957, three years before his son Kim Jong Il began his studies at the school's College of Economics.

student. These sources also state that Kim spent time working at the Puongyang Textile Machine Works, was involved in leading his fellow students in work on the expansion of a major highway, and took part in military camping and exercises. Supposedly, he took part in these military training exercises on the same level as other students, kept to a strict schedule, and ate the same meals as the other students. He was portrayed as an inspirational leader among the other students; one who led his peers to work hard, to think of themselves as revolutionaries, and to prepare themselves accordingly.

In addition to his academic and extracurricular pursuits, several sources credit him with writing 1,500 books, speeches, and other works during his university days. This particular report appears extremely unlikely, because he would have needed to average more than one written work a day for the years he was at the university. Most college students, with all of their academic responsibilities, do not have time to read at that rate, let alone do that much actual writing.

Other accounts are far different than those from official channels, such as reports that Kim spent a fair amount of time during his university years drinking, chasing girls, and partying. Additionally, several sources indicate that, from the time he entered the university, which had been named for his father, Kim Jong Il was not even addressed by his own name. He was called Premier's Son. Special agents were assigned to protect him, and he received special tutoring in all his subjects, from economics and politics to history, philosophy, and languages.

His tutors were not other students or teaching assistants. Kim was tutored by some of the most outstanding professors in their fields. It is rumored that many of his college papers were either revised by his tutors before they were turned in or actually written by his tutors. Official and unofficial sources differ over Kim's undergraduate dissertation. Officially, Kim managed to write this paper in a little over one month. However, some sources credit Jeon Yong Shik, Ph.D., Kim's economics advisor, with ghostwriting this paper.

One important event that occurred in Kim's family during his university years was his father's remarriage in 1963. This marriage resulted in several half-siblings for Kim. Privately, he complained that his father was so busy living up to being the Great Leader that he had little time left for him. The elder Kim's involvement with his new family probably left him with even less time for his firstborn son. Nevertheless, Kim Jong Il worked to gain his

Pyongyang, North Korea

Pyongyang is the capital city of North Korea and the home of Kim Jong Il, the leader of the country. With a population of about four million, it is the largest city in North Korea. It lies on the Taedong River in the south central region of North Korea. Legend has it the city was founded in 2333 B.C. Over the centuries, Pyongyang has been known by several names. According to some sources, it was founded as Wanggomsong and later may have been called Sogyong. The city has also been called Ryugyong, Capital of Willows, because of its numerous willow trees. Pyongyang has been completely rebuilt since the Korean Conflict. It is divided into four counties and nineteen wards.

The skyline of Pyongyang, the capital city of North Korea, rises from the banks of the Taedong River.

father's attention and to please him. On vacations from school, Kim often accompanied his father on government tours and, according to official sources, wrote his thesis about his father's socialist agriculture program.

It was also during his university years that Kim first became interested in motion pictures. He was so fascinated by them that nearly every day he went to the Central Film Distribution Center in downtown Pyongyang. The premier's son was in the center so frequently that the company set up a special viewing room for Kim and his friends. The North Korean film industry was very poor up to the 1960s. Most of its films were about patriots from ordinary life, like nurses and steel workers, reciting dull speeches about their dedication to the Communist Party. These were the films the general public was allowed to see. Kim found these boring. Instead, he watched Soviet movies and movies from Europe and the United States, movies other Koreans were not allowed to see. In fact, had Kim not been in training to become his father's political successor, many believe he would have become a movie producer. However, that choice was not his to make. Kim's father already had his son's political future planned down to the last detail.

In either 1963 or 1964, depending on the source, Kim graduated from Kim Il Sung University with a degree in political economy. His first job after university was with the central committee of the Korean Workers Party, first as a ministerial assistant, and later as a senior official in the propaganda and agitation department. One of his duties was to ensure party activities did not stray from the ideals set by his father.

Some of Kim's duties brought him into contact with the Central Radio and TV Broadcasting Committee. Through this association, Kim met a cameraman. The man had been a war orphan and was a recent newlywed. Prompted by either generosity or to gain favor with his father though positive publicity, Kim took the man to a nice-looking apartment building and gifted him and his new bride with the keys and legal documents to a new apartment: "Now, take it, it is the occupation certificate. I could not allow myself to give you an old house because yours is a new family... Go in and see whether you like it."[6]

The hammer, pen, and sickle symbols of the Korean Workers' Party rise from a memorial tower in Pyongyang. Kim Jong Il became involved with the party's administrative workings after his graduation from Kim Il Sung University in 1963 or 1964.

Personal Relationships

Due to the secrecy that surrounds much of Kim's personal life, actual dates and relationships are somewhat conflicting and muddled. According to some sources, Kim married his first wife, Hong Il Chun, in 1966. She later became vice minister of education. The two are believed to have divorced in 1971.

About this same time, Kim became reacquainted with Sung Hae Rim, a young woman he had first met in high school. She was now a popular movie actress in the North Korean film industry, and he met her again while on a tour of a movie studio. Some say Kim fell in love with the young woman even though she was already married and had a child. By some accounts, Kim forced her to leave her husband to live with him, but other sources say she was genuinely fond of Kim and left her husband willingly. However, despite Kim's privileged status, they could not be seen in public as a couple. Since she was six years his senior and had been previously married, their relationship had to remain a quiet, private one. Even though he was an adult, Kim Jong Il feared his father's reaction if he found out about the relationship. He knew he had to stay in his father's favor if he hoped to be the next leader of his country. According to Sung's sister, to keep the relationship a secret, Kim moved her to one of his more secluded homes. In 1971 she bore him a son. He was named Kim Jong Nam. Ultimately, Sung suffered from a number of nervous disorders and was sent to Moscow for treatment. Her condition grew worse, and she finally died in Russia in 2002.

Despite Kim's efforts to hide this relationship, in the early 1970s, his father found out. As expected, he strongly disapproved and made plans of his own to put an end to this relationship. The elder Kim ordered his son to marry the daughter of one of his senior military officials. Her name was Kim Young Sook. She became his "official" wife and bore him a daughter, Kim Sol Song. Little is known about this daughter, who is not involved in politics.

Working His Way through the Ranks

The late 1960s were apparently a very busy time for Kim Jong Il. One of his duties was providing propaganda on the doctrines and principles of his father's regime for the people of North Korea. He wrote several papers about economics. In some of these papers, he cautioned against making money and other material gains—the main focus of economic growth and development of the country. He also traveled the country, giving speeches about making changes in Korean industries of that time. These were not his

A mural from a movie studio in North Korea depicts Kim Jong Il overseeing a film shoot. His keen interest in cinema led him to develop his nation's film industry into a key propaganda tool, and he produced several films dramatizing his father's experiences and ideals.

only responsibilities. He believed some people in key positions of authority involved with his country's military were deliberately misinterpreting state orders and his father's directives, and these people were a threat to the Workers' Party's influence over the military. He had the officers he believed responsible for these supposed infractions removed from their positions. Additionally, he took an active role in the construction of military facilities, such as the headquarters of the Fifth Corps and the Pyongyang garrison, an underground bunker with state-of-the-art lighting, water and ventilation systems, and living quarters for the military personnel.

He also made use of his interest in the cinema and the fine arts. He believed that improving the Korean film industry would help improve other art forms in his country. He encouraged artists to develop new works, outside of traditional Korean art forms. Some of his own earlier efforts included taking some of his father's writings from the World War II era and turning them into films. The first such film, produced in 1967, when Kim was still in his mid-twenties, was *Five Guerrilla Brothers*. This was the first of a number of films to focus on Kim Il Sung's leadership in the anti-Japanese movement.

However, Kim's direction of Korea's film industry came with specific guidelines. He demanded that all films promote and develop his father's ideals. To do this, he decreed that films should fall into one of three categories: (1) the anti-Japanese efforts of Kim Il Sung, such as the film, *Five Guerrilla Brothers*; (2) the Korean War, for example the film, *Unsung Heroes*; and (3) films to inspire people to work enthusiastically for the good of the party, such as *The Path to Awakening*. Through this form of propaganda, Kim intended to improve the movie industry while keeping it strictly in line with the government policy of honoring Kim Sung Il and the unity of the Workers' Party.

Producers and directors who followed these guidelines stayed on Kim Jong Il's good side. Those who suggested anything that deviated from Kim's orders faced severe consequences. For instance if a director in the North Korean film industry suggested using the methods of European directors, this person risked being labeled an anti-party counterrevolutionary and an enemy of the state. At the very least, this label cost him his job.

The writers who wrote the screenplays for Kim Jong Il's movies also had to contend with demanding working conditions. Several stories from official channels recount Kim Jong Il's dedication to his father and to his own work in the film industry. For instance, while working on the screenplay for the movie, *Sea of Blood*, based on one of Kim Il Sung's writings, the writers sometimes worked far into the night. Very late one evening when they were about to lay aside their work and go to bed, Kim Jong Il sent for them and asked for any other manuscripts they had. Because it was nearly three o'clock in the morning, one of the writers suggested that Kim should get at least a few hours' rest.

Kim supposedly responded:

> ...You know, the President [Kim Il Sung] wrote this celebrated work, sitting up all night for several nights, taking time off in the intervals of the grim, bloody struggle against the Japanese. In that case, how can we allow ourselves to write the screen version of that masterpiece, taking as much rest and sleep as we want, satisfied with our comfortable conditions? I prefer to work in the peaceful, small hours. Give me the manuscripts you've written, please.[7]

The writers were so inspired by his words that they remained at their desks, writing many more hours, before finally falling asleep over their work. Awakened by the sound of splashing, one of the writers walked to the restroom, where he observed Kim Jong Il splashing his face with cold water to revive himself. According to the story, the writers were totally awed by this degree of dedication.

Sea of Blood premiered in 1969, followed by *The Fate of a Self-defense Corps Man* in 1970. Another official story, demonstrating Kim's kindness and consideration toward those working in the film industry, centers around the filming of the latter movie. This story was filmed on location in the Pochonbo Mountains, the far northern part of the country where the weather was quite cold. He sent enough warm clothing, blankets, food, and medicine to take care of every person involved in the filming. The propaganda department made certain that Kim Jong Il's acts of generosity were well publicized.

The Korean Workers' Party

Officially founded in August 1948, the North Korean Workers' Party is the controlling political party in North Korea. Numbering more than three million members as of 1990, the decision-making body of the party is called the Central Committee. From this committee is chosen the thirty-member Political Bureau, or Politbureau. The next rung up the political ladder is the five-member standing committee. The top position is that of Secretary General of the Central Committee. This position is currently held by Kim Jong II. The Workers' Party controls the government, the military, and all media, including television, newspapers, and radio.

Kim, however, also placed enormous pressure on the film crews by pushing these films quickly through production. For instance, a movie that would normally require a year to film and edit was completed in about forty days. This required extremely long workdays on the part of the film crews. Kim believed that high-quality films could be produced in shorter periods of time. Despite the stress this inflicted on the film crews, these efforts paid off. Even people outside the country noticed the improvement in the quality of North Korean films.

About this same time, Kim took on an active role in opera productions in his country, starting with an opera version of the film, *Sea of Blood*. Supposedly, he studied more than 150 songs in order to select the music for this three-act opera. The opera opened in Pyongyang in July 1971. Even a former insider of the Kim regime who later defected to South Korea spoke highly of the production: "Everyone in the audience became deeply moved and stood to applaud Kim Jong Il."[8]

Kim Jong Il's propaganda goals extended beyond movies and opera into dance, plays, orchestra, and other art forms as well. "Works which do not cater to the Party's requirements are of no use at all,"[9] he stated.

Developing a Reputation

From the time he completed college and entered government service, official government and party-approved biographical sources portrayed Kim Jong Il as a brilliant, gifted, inspiring, and benevolent young man—all excellent traits for a future leader. Some reports outside official government sources, however, have been far less flattering. Milder reports allude to Kim as being self-protecting and a self-promoter. Reports of his conceit and arrogance as a young man clash strongly with official reports of his modesty and humility. For instance, in the mid-1960s, Kim worked in his father's military bodyguard organization, with the rank of major. Apparently, he had frequent clashes and disagreements with the head of the Bodyguard Bureau. Some say he was so impressed with himself that he gave out advice unrequested to hear himself talk.

Others are considerably more direct in their descriptions of some of the North Korean dictator's personal habits. For instance, some of Kim's former bodyguards describe him as both a heavy drinker and a heavy smoker, a man prone to excesses, even at the risk of his health. Early in his life, these excesses also extended to gourmet foods and fast cars. At least one account claims Kim was injured in an automobile accident as a young man. Supposedly, he had been driving at the time of the accident. Following the accident, he disappeared from public view for a time. Because of his disappearance, rumors flew. According to some stories, the collision, caused by his reckless driving, had left him a vegetable. Other rumors suggested that he was dead. Finally, gossip was dispelled, because by 1979, he again appeared in public.

In addition to enjoying the excesses made possible by being the son of the most powerful man in North Korea, some indicate that by the time he was a young adult, Kim had already developed a reputation for ruthlessness and something of a cruel streak. Other observers describe him as an extremely ambitious young man, but not especially bloodthirsty. Some sources, however, say he was not above looking on as brutal interrogations were conducted.

Accounts vary on this degree of cruelty. From bullying behavior as a child, some detractors say Kim, though not dirtying his own hands, did not hesitate to order others to do away with his rivals or others who had fallen from his favor. A former confidant of Kim's who later left North Korea told an especially gruesome story. A government secretary told his wife of Kim's drunken, immoral behavior. Being a person of high moral standards, the secretary's wife sent a letter to Kim's father, asking him to discipline his son for such behavior. Kim Il Sung never received the letter; instead, it fell into the hands of Kim Jong Il, who had the woman brought before him, condemned her as a counterrevolutionary, and had her shot. This was meant as a warning to others who might be tempted to speak publicly of his private activities or criticize him in any way.

Despite these alleged traits, though, Kim worked to develop a number of habits that would be useful to any future leader, whether of a dictatorship or a democracy. Unlike people in positions of authority in many dictatorships, who isolate themselves from news of other nations, Kim made efforts to become well informed about the world outside of his country. He watched news programs to learn what was happening in other countries and stay up-to-date on current events around the world. He could also, if it would benefit him, display charming social skills to visitors from other countries. In short, depending on the source of information, young Kim Jong Il had not one reputation, but several. Whichever reputation represented the real Kim Jong Il, though, people in his inner circle knew to watch what they said not only in his presence, but also away from him.

Chapter 3

Grooming for Power

According to a number of people who knew him, Kim Jong Il was extremely focused on his political future, even as a young man. He also did everything he could to impress his father with his earnestness and dedication to upholding his father's political beliefs. To some officials in the North Korean government at that time, he must have come across as a conceited upstart, especially when he lectured those who were supposed to be his superiors about how to do their jobs. There was little they could do about it, because Kim's father was the leader of the entire country. Despite the fact that he was his father's firstborn son, and a strong contender to be his political successor, Kim was by no means assured the job. In fact, there were several among his father's inner circle who were at least as qualified, or probably even more qualified, than Kim Jong Il to succeed Kim Il Sung as the leader of the country, when the time came. Being named his father's successor required careful planning and maneuvering on Kim's part.

Jockeying for Power

Kim Jong Il had been laying the groundwork to become his father's successor for years, traveling with his father, producing operas and motion pictures honoring his father, and promoting his father's political philosophies at every opportunity. In short,

Kim did everything he could to flatter his father and play to his ego.

For instance, when Kim Il Sung turned sixty, Kim Jong Il planned and threw what was possibly the most opulent, lavish celebration in the country's history, complete with pageants and parades. No effort was too extreme to win his father's favor. He also established the Kim Il Sung Institute of Health and Longevity, a research program he created to prolong his father's life. Instead of laboratory rats, though, human beings served as test subjects for the experimental drugs and diets under research.

A public mural of Kim Il Sung benevolently leading his happy followers is an example of the tireless propaganda organized by Kim Jong Il to promote his father's authority and ideals.

Kim's tireless, relentless promotion of his father developed into a near religion in North Korea, what is called a *personality cult*. This is when the leader of a country is raised to an almost mythic heroic image by individuals, the media, and the political party in power. In short, any time his father was praised and cheered, it was in Kim Jong Il's interest to be out in front, acting as the head cheerleader.

Despite being the son of the Great Leader, several people stood between Kim and his goal of becoming the next leader of the Democratic People's Republic of Korea, also known as North Korea. Among them were his father's brother, Kim Yong Ju; his own half-brother, Kim Pyong Il; and even his stepmother, Kim Song Ae, whom people said he despised. In fact, she is seldom, if ever, referred to in any of Kim's official biographies.

Rivalry developed with his uncle about the time Kim Jong Il graduated from college and began working for the Communist Party in his country. Before this, Kim Yong Ju appeared to be the first in line to be Kim Il Sung's successor. He had many supporters in influential places, including Kim Song Ae, Kim Il Sung's second wife. Most of the rivalry revolved around the Kim Il Sung personality cult. Kim Jong Il and Kim Yong Ju constantly tried to outdo each other, elevating Kim Sung Il to a higher and higher pedestal, almost to the point of raising Kim Sung Il to the status of a god-king.

Kim Il Sung was aware that his brother and his son often clashed. He tried to restore a measure of peace by having his son transferred for a short time from the Central Committee in Pyongyang to the party chapter in North Hamgyong Province, where Kim Jong Il worked with Kim Guk Tae. Kim Guk Tae was the local party boss and the son of a well-known anti-Japanese guerrilla general. Young Kim returned to Pyongyang in 1966, where he could better keep an eye on his prospects for succeeding his father. In 1973, through political maneuvering, he took the position of party organization secretary from his uncle.

He even went so far as to purge the memoirs written by some of his father's old comrades, memoirs that Kim Il Sung, himself, had originally encouraged his former comrades in arms to write about themselves. Kim Jong Il destroyed these books because he

A marble likeness of Kim Il Sung watches over the Supreme People's Assembly in Pyongyang. One of many such statues, paintings, and other tributes to the North Korean leader commissioned by Kim Jong Il in order to extol his father's supremacy.

felt they detracted from his father's personality cult. Not only did he eliminate writings, he also removed party leaders, like Baek Nam Woon, who was at one time a respected scholar and leader. Toward the end of the 1960s, it was reported that Kim Jong Il removed Baek from his job and imprisoned him in a concentration camp, where he later died. Such drastic action apparently did not require actual proof of disloyalty. Although he had never participated in any campaigns against Kim Il Sung, Baek was imprisoned based on less than flattering comments about the Great Leader that Baek may or may not have made.

Kim Jong Il's role as propagandist placed him in the perfect position for someone who wanted to climb the career ladder to the top. He promoted total, unwavering dedication to the rule of one man, his father. In fact, he elevated his father above the Workers' Party, which had put him in power. For example, he commissioned plaster busts to be made of his father, which he had placed in prominent locations throughout the country. He also changed the name of the Study Hall of the History of the Workers' Party of Korea to Study Hall of Comrade Kim Il Sung's Revolutionary History. No effort to extol his father was too great or too small to escape Kim's obsessive attention. For instance, he objected to the way a list of names of party officials, including his father's, had been typed. He had the list retyped, leaving a space between Kim Il Sung's name and the rest of the names on the list. He also had his father's name printed in larger type than the names of the other officials. He described his reason for doing this to one of the officials: "Think. It's because the sun shines that the planets shed their light, isn't it? As we could not draw the sun and the planets in the same size, so we would never write down the name of the leader and the names of his men in the same size."[10]

Political Climate in North Korea

Ironically, Kim's efforts to promote the hero worship of his father overshadowed some of the original principles of *juche*, the political philosophy his father had set forth in North Korea. Basically, the term, "juche," means self-reliance or self-dependence—a self-sufficient economy, totally independent foreign policy, and a self-reliant defense position. According to Kim's interpretation of juche, to achieve this total self-reliance, the people had to be ready to make personal sacrifices, live a life without luxuries, and be totally united in patriotism. Evidently, the Kim political regime supported the intent in word rather than in deed. The officials in power did not set examples by denying themselves the finer things of life. In fact, they lived quite lavishly in large homes, ate the best food, and drove luxurious cars. In addition, according to Kim's interpretation, for juche to be successful, the people must have independence in both thought and politics, and the policies of the country should reflect the will of the people. Yet, at the same time, the people were expected to give absolute loyalty to the leader and to the party. In his country, Kim's interpretation of the juche system became a higher priority than education. This thought process has been ingrained into the people of North Korea in a number of ways, from speeches to the state-controlled media organizations.

Realistically, it did not appear that the people had many choices in how they thought or spoke. In fact, human rights organizations claim that the opinions of the citizens of North Korea have had no bearing on the decision-making process under the Kim regime. Additionally, the meaning of juche had been so changed by the Kim regime that the one-time top North Korean juche theorist, Hwang Jang Yop, defected to South Korea. He still believed in the principles of juche, but he felt that these principles were not being practiced by those in power in North Korea.

According to many sources, a heavy cloud of suspicion, distrust, and oppression has hung over the entire country for decades. The Kim regime has for years controlled all aspects of its citizens' lives. For example, the State Security Department keeps all citizens and government officials under strict surveillance through the use of informants. The government also monitors telephone and other communications systems. Furthermore, all media communications, including radio, television, and news-papers, are under government control. Additionally, although freedom of religion is guaranteed under the constitution of North

Cult of Personality

When the leader of a country is turned into a larger-than-life figure through the manipulation of mass media, the resulting pseudo-religious fervor is called a cult of personality, or personality cult. This phenomenon can sometimes occur in democracies, but is usually observed in dictatorships. Examples include Germany's Adolph Hitler, Italy's Benito Mussolini, and China's Chairman Mao. Historic film footage shows huge parades and ceremonies honoring these men who were literally worshipped by the people of their country. North Korea is generating a second-generation personality cult. Its first was that of Kim Il Sung. Since his death, his son, Kim Jong Il has been elevated to a similar god-king-like status.

Thousands of North Korean children perform at a rally in Pyongyang in honor of Kim Il Sung, who along with Kim Jong Il has been elevated, through relentless propaganda and promotion, to an object of worship among the North Korean people.

Figures depicting the might of North Korean workers stand before the Tower of the Juche Idea, a monument in Pyongyang that promotes the political philosophy followed by Kim Il Sung, which dictates an ideal of self reliance, sacrifice, and unity for his nation and its people.

Korea, it does not actually exist. Church groups are essentially underground operations, because church members and leaders know they may be imprisoned or killed for elevating any belief above the cult of personality or for having contact with overseas religious groups.

Under the younger Kim's direction, even some major points of North Korean official history appear to have been rewritten. This Kim-edited version of North Korean history further elevated Kim Il Sung's stature and the greatness of North Korea while downplaying the actual roles of other nations that had been allies of the country. For instance, rather than granting China recognition for its service to North Korea during the Korean War, the official interpretation is that a few volunteers from China assisted North Korea. Needless to say, these actions did not improve the relationship between the governments of China and North Korea.

As if these maneuvers were not enough, Kim went even further in isolating his country and its people from surrounding countries. At one time, visitors from communist countries, such as China or the Soviet Bloc countries, could travel freely in North Korea. By the mid-1960s and early 1970s, though, visitors from formerly friendly communist countries were restricted as to where they could go within North Korea and were allowed very little contact with the people. Additionally, any North Korean officials who were thought to have pro-Chinese or pro-Soviet beliefs were removed from positions of power.

As more time passed under the guidance of the Kim regime, North Korea moved further away politically from its Chinese and Soviet mentors, on whom the country had previously depended for trade. According to official government policy, Marxism and Leninism were useful doctrines of communism in their day, but their day had passed, and juche, or Kim's interpretation of juche, was the only effective means of enhancing the future of communist society. Beyond that, Kim Jong Il suggested that the juche ideology be renamed Kim Il Sungism. According to Kim, this philosophy was superior to all other thought systems, including Leninism and Marxism. Though denied other religions, the citizens of North Korea were essentially expected to worship Kim Il Sung.

Juche

Juche is a national belief in self-reliance. According to Kim Il Sung, the late North Korean dictator who died in 1994, *juche*, or *chuch'e*, "...means the independent stance of rejecting dependence on others and of using one's own powers, believing in one's own strength, and displaying the revolutionary spirit of self-reliance."

During the first ten years following North Korean liberation from Japan, the country was governed according to Marxism and Leninism, the political doctrines of the Soviet Union and China. Beginning in the mid-1950s, Kim Il Sung began promoting the principle of juche. By the mid-1970s, Kim Il Sung had declared Marxism and Leninism outdated and obsolete, and juche was North Korea's political ideology. His son, Kim Jong Il, changed the term juche to Kim Il Sungism, in honor of his father.

Source: GlobalSecurity.org, "Juche: Self-Reliance or Self-Dependence," April 27, 2005. www.globalsecurity.org/military/world/dprk/juche.htm.</SB>

In addition to the Kim regime isolating North Korea and its people from former allies, the former allies were dealing with problems of their own, which had an economic impact on North Korea. China and the Soviet Bloc countries were experiencing internal problems. The Soviet Bloc countries included the Soviet Union, Bulgaria, Czechoslovakia, East Germany, Hungary, Poland, Romania, and Albania. They were providing fewer and fewer exports to North Korea. Despite its official policy of self-sufficiency, North Korea needed those exports. While elite government officials still had favorite foods and luxury items flown in for themselves, because the wealth of the country was in their hands and at their disposal, the working class people of North Korea, who often could not afford basic necessities, suffered hardships.

Captive Entertainment

Despite the hardships endured by the citizens of North Korea, Kim Jong Il denied himself nothing. He enjoyed special foods, expensive cars, a huge library of motion pictures, and he owned a number of mansions. Whatever he wanted, he had it imported from other countries. Sometimes, this included people; people who were brought into North Korea, whether they wanted to be there or not. One such story concerns a famous South Korean actress. According to some sources, Kim ordered his agents stationed in South Korea to kidnap popular actress, Choi Eun Hee, and her ex-husband, film director Shin Sang Ok. To do this, they first lured the actress to Hong Kong, supposedly to discuss a film role. She was kidnapped and taken to North Korea by boat, an eight-day ordeal. When she arrived, Kim Jong Il supposedly met her on the dock to welcome her to the Democratic People's Republic of Korea. Choi was afraid to ask why she had been brought to his country by force. Although a virtual prisoner, Choi was provided with luxurious surroundings.

What Kim wanted from Choi was her talent and her knowledge of the motion picture industry. She was made to study Kim Il Sung, Kim Jong Il, and the revolution as interpreted by Kim Jong Il. Despite the fact he had had her taken by force, Kim attempted to win Choi's favor by taking her to movies, musicals, and operas. He had her watch films and asked her opinion of them. For reading material, he provided her with a three-volume biography of Kim Hong Jik, Kim Il Sung's father. She also watched Kim's movies, *Sea of Blood* and *The Flower Girl*. She was impressed by the films, but not altogether sure how much Kim actually had to do with their making.

In the meantime, Shin, who had remained on friendly terms with his ex-wife, tried to learn what had happened to her. Six months after her disappearance, he went to Hong Kong, where she had last been seen, to get information about her disappearance. Like Choi, Shin was shanghaied by Kim's operatives, who slipped a bag over his head and hustled him off to North Korea. First, he was taken to Pyongyang, where he, too, was provided with luxury accommodations. However, no one would tell him

South Korean actress Choi Eun Hee, left, and her husband, director Shin Sang Ok, detail their ordeal of captivity and escape after being held in North Korea for more than five years so that Kim Jong Il could use their talents and expertise to benefit his country's film industry.

where Choi was or what had happened to her. During his earliest years of captivity in North Korea, Shin attempted to escape twice. These attempts angered Kim, and Shin was put in prison for his disobedience to Kim's wishes. During his time in jail, he endured physical suffering and other hardships. For instance, after waking in the morning, he was made to hold his arms over his head until breakfast time. He also had to sit in uncomfortable positions for hours at a time and could not speak with other prisoners. Finally, Shin wrote a letter that convinced Kim that he had seen the error of his ways. Shin was released from jail.

Five years after they were first kidnapped, Shin and Choi were reunited. Surprisingly to both Shin and Choi, Kim apologized for keeping them away from each other. In fact, Kim encouraged them to remarry. Kim also announced that he was appointing Shin as his film advisor. After the wedding celebration, Shin and Choi were set to work, watching and critiquing films. Most of the films were from communist countries, but a few had been made in the United States. Kim would phone the couple daily to see if they were in good health or needed anything. This was a considerable turnaround from Shin's time in jail.

Additionally, Shin was provided with a 2.5 million dollar Swiss bank account to finance filmmaking projects. He made twenty films, many of them propaganda-inspired, while a captive guest of Kim Jong Il. Over time, Shin came to respect Kim's knowledge of films, however, there remained the issue that Shin and Choi had been kidnapped and were being forced to stay in North Korea, seldom allowed to communicate with people from outside the country. In his own way, Kim reasoned with them about the necessity of their isolation. "It is not propitious to talk about it truthfully,"[11] he said of the kidnapping. He concocted a script for Shin and Choi to use with people outside of North Korea. They were to say that they had no freedom or democracy in South Korea, so they had come to North Korea to have real freedom to pursue their artistic endeavors. Eventually, they were allowed to leave country, but only one at a time, and that person was closely guarded. Because of this, both Shin and Choi stuck to Kim's prepared script. They said that they had gone to North Korea voluntarily.

The pair finally won Kim's confidence, though, and were allowed to leave the country together to travel to special events. They were still closely watched, however. Their escape from Kim and North Korea was as dramatic as a scene from any action film. In 1986 they traveled to a film festival in Vienna, Austria. While on a taxi ride to the festival, their cab got several car lengths ahead of the taxi in which their guards were traveling. They reached an intersection. Instead of turning right, toward the location of the festival, they had their taxi turn left and drive them to the United States Embassy. When the guards arrived at the festival site and realized that Choi and Shin were not there, they radioed the taxi driver and asked him where he was taking the pair. Choi and Shin had bribed their driver not to tell their guards where they were. Unable to find a place to stop, the taxi dropped them down the road from the embassy. "We tried to run as fast as we could, but it felt like we were in some sort of slow motion movie. Finally, we burst through the embassy's doors and asked for asylum,"[12] Shin said. For the first time since their abduction, they were able to speak truthfully of their years as forced guests of North Korea and Kim Jong Il.

Family and Relationships

The abductions of a famous Korean film star and director were not the only issues Kim tried to keep quiet. According to sources, he has always been secretive about his personal life. However, due to intelligence sources and the reports of North Koreans who have defected, bits and pieces of information about his private life have come to light. For instance, depending on the source of information, Kim has somewhere between eleven and thirteen children by his various wives and girlfriends. Since family information is so heavily guarded, it would be very difficult, if not impossible, to determine how many of Kim's children are sons and how many are daughters.

Following his earlier marriages and subsequent relationships, Kim entered into a relationship with a well-known North Korean dancer, Koh Young Hui. She was much favored by Kim Jong Il and, for a time, actually took over the role of first lady of North Korea. She reportedly died in 2004 of cancer. According to reports, Kim was deeply saddened by her death. After a time, though, Kim became involved with his personal secretary, Kim Ok.

Little, if any, public information exists on some of his children, and, of those whose names are known, few details are available.

Kim Jong Il poses with his oldest son, Kim Jong Nam, seated right, and other relatives in this 1981 photo. Details about the Korean leader's private life are highly guarded, with most information on his family coming from intelligence sources and accounts from North Korean defectors.

As previously described, Kim reportedly had a daughter with Kim Young Sook, Kim Sol Song, who stays out of the public eye. Kim's first son, Kim Jong Nam, was born to actress, Sung Hae Rim, who reportedly died in Moscow sometime in 2002. Kim Jong Nam was thought to be his father's favorite and was a frontrunner to succeed him in power until Japanese officials caught him trying to enter Japan on a fake passport. Supposedly, he was attempting to visit Tokyo Disneyland. This incident caused North Korea a great deal of embarrassment, because it made Kim's son and heir apparent look silly and irresponsible.

Kim had two sons, both born in the 1980s, by Koh Young Hui. They are Kim Jong Chol and Kim Jong Un. The few known facts about Kim Jong Chol include his love of professional basketball, a trait he appears to have inherited from his father, and that, at one time, he went to school in Switzerland. Kim Johng Un, the younger of the two, looks much like his father, and some sources indicate that, since Kim Jong Nam's fall from favor, Kim Jong Un might someday become his father's successor. Before Kim Jong Il needed a successor, though, he first needed to attain the top political position in North Korea. Though elderly and in frail health, his father was still the leader of the country.

Chapter 4

Dear Leader

In the summer of 1994, Kim Il Sung traveled to his retreat in the Myohyang Mountains to escape the heat of the city. En route to his summer villa, he stopped to inspect a collective farm. The midday heat had reached 100 degrees Fahrenheit (37.78 degrees Celsius), and the visit had left the eighty-two-year-old weak and tired. Spending the day in the extreme heat had been too much for Kim, and he suffered a massive heart attack at his villa late that same evening. His chief secretary found him face down on the floor beside his bed. Doctors were summoned, but due to heavy rain in the area, they could not be transported by air, and the roads were largely impassible. In fact, one helicopter, carrying emergency equipment to Kim's retreat, crashed. The roads were in such bad shape that ground transportation was agonizingly slow. By the time the doctors arrived, Kim Il Sung was beyond help. He was pronounced dead at two in the early morning hours of July 8.

The news of the leader's death was kept quiet for more than twenty-four hours, while government officials planned how they would inform the people. The announcement was finally made in a television statement on July 9: "Our respected fatherly leader who has devoted his whole life to the popular masses' cause of independence and engaged himself in tireless activities for the prosperity of the motherland and happiness of the people, for the reunification of our country and independence of the world, till the last moments of his life, departed from us to our greatest sorrow."[13]

While it appears to be a fact that Kim Il Sung died at his summer retreat, some rumors surround the exact cause of his death. According to one account, a doctor was present when Kim became ill, but his son had fired his regular doctor, claiming that he was too old. Supposedly, the younger doctor was too inexperienced to handle such a serious emergency, and so the elder Kim died before a proper medical team could reach the villa. According to a different account, Kim Il Sung had become furiously angry with his son for sidestepping his order to provide more electrical service to the general public. In fact, he had become so enraged, he had walked out in the middle of a meeting. There is speculation that this upset led to his heart attack. Regardless of the exact cause of the elder Kim's death, though, a successor would be named, and that successor would be Kim Jong Il.

Assuming Leadership

With the exception of the televised funeral, where he was described as looking dazed, silently looking on as others made speeches, Kim was not seen in public for a long period of time after his father's death. Officially, he was in deep mourning, but other speculations rose about his absence. One had to do with his health. Kim had fallen from a horse the previous autumn, and some thought his physical appearance and absence from public might have to do with injuries associated with that accident. Another report indicated that he had fasted for several days prior to his appearance at the funeral so that he would look appropriately pale and wan. Finally, there were rumors of internal power struggles; some believed that if Kim took over, the military might overthrow him. Whatever the purpose, though, he kept a low public profile those first three years after his father's elaborate memorial service.

After a three-year official mourning period, during which time

Kim Jong Il is flanked by mourning government and military officials at the funeral of his father, Kim Il Sung, in July 1994.

the country was basically under his control, Kim Jong Il formally took office. Rather than assuming the office of president, Kim took the title Secretary-General of the North Korean Worker's Party in October 1997. This title had more staying power than that of president. According to the North Korean constitution, the office of president requires elections, whereas the office of secretary-general does not.

As for his other title, Kim had been known as "Dear Leader" since 1991, when his father appointed him supreme commander of the Korean People's Army. Now, he assumed his father's title, "Great Leader." A year after taking over leadership of his country,

Kim announced that his father would be known thereafter as president of the country for eternity. He gave his late father the title "Eternal Leader."

The new leader of North Korea was different from his father in a number of ways. First, there were physical differences. Kim Il Sung was larger than his son and had a deep, rich voice. According to most physical descriptions, Kim Il Sung was about 5 feet, 6 inches tall (1.67m), a little above average for the height of an adult Korean male at that time. Kim Jong Il, however, is only about 5 feet, 2 inches (1.57m), a small man with curly hair. Additionally, although father and son, the backgrounds of Kim Jung Il and his father could not have been more different. Kim Il Sung grew up in dire poverty, fleeing from place to place with his family to escape persecution by the Japanese. As he moved into adulthood, he lived the life of a guerilla fighter, kill or be killed. It was a life of physical hardships; he often slept on the ground and went without food. Kim Jong Il, however, never knew such challenges. The younger Kim had neither experienced the hardships of war nor, despite the fact he had been named head of the military, had any real military experience. He went to the best schools, lived in mansions with staffs of servants to satisfy his every want and whim, drove fine cars, and never missed a meal.

If political conditions in North Korea were oppressive under Kim Il Sung, they became even more so under his son. As the new leader of North Korea, Kim Jong Il was described as being even more ruthless than his father. It is said that from the time he assumed leadership, he micro-managed every element of the government, just as he micro-managed the cult of personality for his father. He established tight control over the daily lives of the North Koreans. Although the country was already steeped in suspicion and distrust, tensions increased to an even higher level when Kim assumed leadership. He increased surveillance of his own party officials. Officials were expected to turn in a list of all of their daily activities to Kim and could not hold meetings without his personal permission. When he did authorize meetings, he often goaded officials into criticizing each other. "He actually enjoys harassing party members,"[14] said a former official who later defected.

Unlike his father, who would call in his senior officials and have discussions with them before deciding policy, whether this was done for show or if he actually incorporated the ideas of his officials or not, Kim made all the decisions for his regime. Every aspect of government was under his tight control. Except for a few family members and friends, Kim trusted no one. In addition to all of the constraints within the country, communications with other countries were so carefully monitored that North Korea was effectively shut off from the rest of the world, an isolated kingdom controlled by one man. Apparently, Kim had much to lose if word

A public mural depicts late North Korean leader Kim Il Sung showing the way to his son, Kim Jong Il, who assumed official control of the country three years after his father's death in 1994, plunging the already isolated, secretive nation into an even deeper level of oppression and paranoia.

got out about the extent of his lavish lifestyle, such as his eight palaces, stables, golf courses, swimming pools, hunting grounds, and Disney land-like amusement parks, for the enjoyment of his personal circle of family and friends. People who have been to his palaces say that the utter luxury and opulence of these mansions and their grounds is beyond imagination.

Although he had known nothing but wealth and privilege throughout his life, as leader of the country, Kim now lived the life of kings and potentates straight from the pages of fairy tales. He had personal staff to attend to his every desire and need, from doctors to dancing troupes. All eight palaces maintain full-time

Kim Jong II's Lavish Lifestyle

While many of his people scramble to find enough food to feed their families, Kim Jong II enjoys the best his country has to offer, and, if he cannot find what he wants in North Korea, he imports it. Kim is known to eat twenty-course dinners. He may wash down such a meal with one of his favorite alcoholic beverages, Hennessy Cognac Paradis, which sells for $650 a bottle. This is about the same amount of money the average North Korean earns in a year.

However, Kim does enjoy some more common foods, such as pizza. His method of making sure he can always have pizza on hand was somewhat extravagant, though. He imported pizza ovens and two chefs. He brought in the chefs to teach his personal chefs how to properly prepare pizza.

Other examples reveal his lavish lifestyle as well. For instance, in 1998, he imported two hundred Class S Mercedes automobiles at a cost of $20 million. He is said to own six villas and mansions outside of North Korea in addition to the homes he owns in his country. He is also reported to have billions of dollars in bank accounts in Switzerland.

staffs, whether Kim is in attendance or not. He amuses himself by riding motorcycles on one of his estates or taking cruises on his personal yacht.

"In [a] real sense, he is the richest man in the world. There are not limits on what he can do. In South Korea there are rich men but I have never seen any facilities here which can rival what Kim has,"[15] said Lee Young Guk, Kim's former bodyguard.

From the beginning of Kim's absolute hold on power, North Korea has been the exact opposite of a democratic country. In a democracy, the leaders are supposed to work for and support the good of the people. However, in North Korea, the people work to support the lavish lifestyle of their leader. The economic gap between the average North Korean and Kim Jong Il is beyond enormous. For example, whereas Kim spends more than half of a million dollars a year on his favorite cognac, a type of liquor, the average North Korean earns the equivalent of only $600 to $900 a year.

Decline in Economy and Living Conditions

Economic problems did not begin when Kim Jong Il took office. His father had experienced a great deal of difficulty managing the economy. In fact, according to a number of economists, the North Korean economy dropped anywhere from 5 percent to 7 percent per year between 1990 and 1997, the year Kim took office.

North Korea has never had a strong economy, and a number of events occurred through the 1980s and 1990s that made matters worse. First, the country lost trade agreements with China and with the Soviet Bloc countries, the former Soviet Union. The Soviet Union demanded cash payment for exports it shipped to North Korea, and North Korea did not have the money to pay them. Then, conditions worsened during the floods of the 1990s, described as the worst in one hundred years. They destroyed most of the crops and flooded the coal mines, which seriously affected energy production. Finally, the flooding was followed by several years of severe drought. This combination of weather disasters resulted in an economy in shambles.

Additionally, the government did not listen to the needs of its people. Because the government carefully monitored the media, neither word of the widespread shortages and other economic problems nor criticism were tolerated. Kim Jong Il's government attempted measures, called shortsighted and rash by some, in an effort to stimulate the economy. For instance, although Kim's government was not responsible for the flooding, the government-ordered felling of huge numbers of trees, apparently under

A North Korean farmer struggles to move his cart across a flood-damaged rice field in 1996. Severe weather and government mismanagement decimated the nation's farmland in the 1990s, resulting in widespread famine among the North Korean people.

Kim's direction, caused added topsoil erosion during the flooding. Flooding and erosion wiped out more 15 percent of the farmable land, causing an estimated $15 billion in damages. With the loss of cropland and lacking grain, energy, and fertilizer; the agricultural output of the country plummeted by nearly 50 percent. People coped by gathering wild roots, greens, herbs, and vegetables, when they could find them. Some were reduced to eating grass, leaves, and bark from trees. Illegal markets, called black markets, appeared throughout the country, where people sold scavenged or stole items to buy what little food was available. As tightly controlled as the government was, though, times were so hard it could do little about these activities.

With flooding, drought, economic mismanagement, and political isolationism; North Korea plunged into a nationwide famine. Their state-run health system collapsed. Hospitals lacked the necessary medicine and equipment to treat patients. Due to a shortage of electricity and chlorine, a chemical used to make water safe to drink, not enough clean drinking and cooking water remained to meet the people's daily needs. The percentage of people who had access to safe drinking water declined from 86 percent to 53 percent.

The decline in living standards dropped the life expectancy of the average North Korean from 73.2 years to 66.8 years. Additionally, the infant mortality rate climbed from 14 to 22.5 deaths per 1,000 live births. Death rates for children under five years of age grew from 27 to 48 per 1,000 children. The drop in vaccines for childhood diseases from 90 percent to 50 percent was a contributor to this fact. Many children and adults suffered from malnutrition, dysentery, and vitamin and iodine deficiencies. As many as 2.5 million North Koreans may have died from a lack of sufficient food or from eating dangerous substances out of desperation.

North Korea was not able to keep up with other countries in industry either. The country became essentially bankrupt and could not pay for goods it imported. Kim blamed many of the economic problems and food shortages on lazy party officials. He condemned his subordinates for the fact that people had little or no food. He absolved himself of any responsibility for economic problems stating, "I cannot solve all the problems...as I have to control important sectors such as the military and the party as well. If I concentrated only on the economy there would be irrecoverable damage to the revolution. The Great Leader told me when he was alive never to be involved in economic projects, just concentrate on the military and the party and leave economics to party functionaries. If I do delve into economics, then I cannot run the party and military effectively."[16]

While Kim's people went without, Kim concentrated on building his armed forces, investing one quarter of the country's Gross Domestic Product (GDP) on the military. The GDP is the total market value of goods, services, and capital produced within a country for a period of time, usually a year. That money was not enough to feed his forces. Food shortages led soldiers to steal from civilians and sometimes desert the army. One soldier who deserted the army and defected to South Korea said that his squad would go on food raids two or three times a month. Officials broadcast messages by television and radio, directing the farmers to provide more food for the military. They actually accused the farmers of hiding food. Officials remained in their offices and relied on the media to issue their directives rather than going out into the field and visiting the farms themselves. Few people received these messages, however, since television and radio require electricity, and there was no electricity in most outlying areas.

Natural disasters and economic mismanagement were not the sole causes of North Korea's economic problems. Internal problems were made worse by economic sanctions. Economic sanctions are the withholding of goods and services. Other countries, upset that North Korea had become involved in nuclear weapons testing and development, imposed these sanctions. The North Koreans even sold some of their weapons to countries that were politically unstable and potentially dangerous to the West, such as Iran. Some world leaders felt that Kim Jong Il and his country were using nuclear weapons as a form of worldwide blackmail.

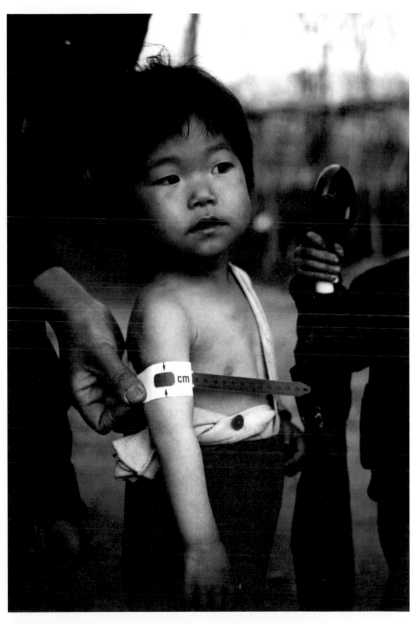

Aid workers in North Korea examine a malnourished child, one of millions of North Koreans who suffered the effects of the nation's severe food shortage during the 1990s, a time when Kim Jong Il increased military spending and indulged in personal luxuries.

A History of Nuclear Conflict

North Korea has a long history of nuclear research and development. The country began its involvement with nuclear programs in the 1960s, during Kim Il Sung's early days in office. Its first plutonium, only five grams, was produced in 1975. Plutonium is a naturally radioactive element. It occurs naturally in uranium, but is usually developed in nuclear reactors. This element is used to produce powerful bombs.

However, in 1985, North Korea signed the Nuclear Nonproliferation Treaty (NPT), agreeing not to produce bombs and to open all nuclear sites for inspection. It was not a free offer, though. The Soviet Union promised to provide North Korea with several larger power reactors for peacetime purposes. Later that same year, North Korea began building a reactor capable of producing seven to ten bombs a year. Similar activities continued until 1987, when North Korea missed its first eighteen-month

Tanks fitted with missiles are part of a parade in Pyongyang in April 1992, a show of North Korea's military might after years of repeatedly violating the terms of the Nuclear Nonproliferation Treaty that it singed in 1985.

Plutonium

Plutonium is a rare radioactive metallic chemical that is extremely toxic. People can become contaminated by this substance from ingesting it in foods, breathing it, or getting it into open wounds. More than one-third of the energy created in most nuclear power plants comes from plutonium. Nuclear weapons testing in the 1950s and 1960s released huge amounts of this toxic substance into the atmosphere. In fact, since 1945, 770 kilograms have been released into the atmosphere as a result of this testing. No chemical process can destroy it, but it can be mixed with radioactive isotopes or uranium to make it useless to terrorist groups.

Despite its use as a weapon of mass destruction, plutonium can also be a helpful, even a life-saving substance. It is used in space probes and was even used at one time to power artificial hearts and pacemakers.

deadline for the beginning of inspections. They were granted an additional eighteen-month extension. They missed their second deadline in 1988, and by 1989, North Korea abandoned all pretense of compliance and openly refused the inspections. Additionally, they were selling scud missiles to Iran. Scuds are relatively small ballistic missiles with motorized guidance systems.

Then, in 1993, a year before Kim Il Sung's death, North Korea completely withdrew from the Nuclear Nonproliferation treaty. That same year, Moscow expelled a North Korean diplomat for attempting to lure Russian scientists to North Korea. North Korea continued their plutonium production, and U.S. intelligence officials said there was a better than 50/50 chance that North Korea possessed one, if not two, bombs.

By 1994, the United States announced its intent of uniting

a number of countries in imposing economic sanctions against North Korea if the country continued to refuse inspections. That same year, when former U.S. president Jimmy Carter met with Kim Il Sung, the North Korean president offered to freeze their nuclear program if the United States joined him in high-level negotiations. However, Kim Il Sung died that year. Kim's death did not end the talks; it merely delayed them. The talks resumed in Geneva, Switzerland, in early August of that same year. Within a week, negotiators outlined an agreement. According to the document, North Korea would abandon gas graphite nuclear plants in favor of lightweight reactor facilities. They also discussed the 8,000 irradiated fuel rods North Korea possessed, its facility that could extract sufficient plutonium from those rods to make several nuclear weapons, and the ever-present issue of inspections.

The inspection issue produced a stalemate. The North Korean representative stated that his country would never submit to inspections that infringed on national sovereignty, whereas the U.S. negotiators insisted that such inspections had to be part of the agreement. Finally, the North Korean negotiator said that they might concede to inspections after his country received about 80 percent of the light-water reactors it had been promised. Then, on October 21, 1994, the agreement was signed. According to the terms, the United States would supply North Korea with 500,000 tons of fuel to supplement their energy needs and would additionally provide light-water reactors by 2003. For its part, North Korea agreed with the terms for inspections and promised to dismantle its existing nuclear operations.

Although the country was in the midst of an official three-year mourning period and had signed an agreement tentatively agreeing to inspections, North Korea continued to pursue nuclear activities. They supplied Iran with additional scud missiles and announced they would no longer respect the demilitarized zone between North and South Korea. In fact, in 1996, North Korea held three days of military exercises in the zone. Additionally, a North Korean submarine, believed to be involved in spying on its neighbor to the south, ran aground on the South Korean coastline. South Korea demanded, and received, an apology from North Korea for the incident.

A North Korean satellite soars into space atop a three-stage rocket in October 1998, provoking international concern that the nation had the capacity to launch nuclear weapons that could reach distant countries, including the United States.

The next year, one of Kim Jong Il's top advisors defected to South Korea. He informed South Korean officials that based on his knowledge of North Korean nuclear activities, the country had enough nuclear weapons to use against both South Korea and Japan.

Signed agreements apparently had little effect on North Korean production of plutonium and missiles. In the summer of 1998 North Korean representatives stated that they would continue to build and export missiles with nuclear capabilities. In fact, in 1998, North Korea launched a three-stage rocket, carrying a satellite. Intelligence sources state that such a rocket could reach the United States. Additionally, intelligence sources reported that North Korea was building a large underground facility, one that might be a reprocessing plant or a nuclear reactor. By the summer of 1999 sources reported that North Korea had enough weapon-grade plutonium to create several nuclear warheads.

As for Kim Jong Il's role in North Korea's nuclear development, it appeared that the small man and his tiny country intended to take on the rest of the world or at least hold it hostage by constant threats of nuclear retaliation. Under Kim Jong Il's leadership, North Korea continues to oppose other countries in a virtual ping-pong game of agreements and broken promises, an ongoing situation that causes other countries to distrust Kim and his motives.

Chapter 5

Kim's Legacy

Although Kim Jong Il is not responsible for starting nuclear research and development programs that were begun while his father was in control of the country, Kim has perpetuated them. Despite numerous serious problems within his country, Kim Jong Il promises to cease producing nuclear weapons and nuclear-capable weapons, but then violates the agreements. Countries close to North Korea, like South Korea and Japan, are concerned for their own safety. They believe that a nuclear attack against their countries is a real possibility. Other countries are angry at what they see as Kim's brash disregard for any agreements; some see any agreements made with North Korea as essentially worthless and consider time spent on negotiations wasted.

One reason for Kim's behavior might have to do with his own background. Since childhood, he has been denied nothing. He is never contradicted within his own country; and, as dictator, Kim has total command over North Korea. He controls both the government and the media. This being the case, some believe that Kim feels as entitled to have his own way outside his country as he does within it. Although North Korea is quite small in comparison to other countries, Kim knows that his country controls a legitimate threat. That threat is the North Korean potential to harm other countries with its nuclear weapons.

As to the state of his mental and physical health, because Kim keeps any mention of his personal affairs under tight control, it is often difficult to separate fact from fiction about the leader of this tiny country. Some say he is a brilliant strategist, whereas others insist he is a madman. Either way, nuclear weapons at the disposal of this man is an issue that governments around the world watch closely.

Concessions and Threats

An ongoing insecure relationship exists between Kim, the United States, and other countries over these nuclear issues. Kim Jong Il shows no sign of breaking the pattern of making and then backing out of nuclear agreements, begun when his father was in power. For instance, in 2002, North Korean officials admitted

A cooling pond at a nuclear facility in Yongbyon, North Korea, contains spent nuclear fuel rods that United Nations inspectors were monitoring in the mid-1990s to ensure they were not used in the production of nuclear weapons.

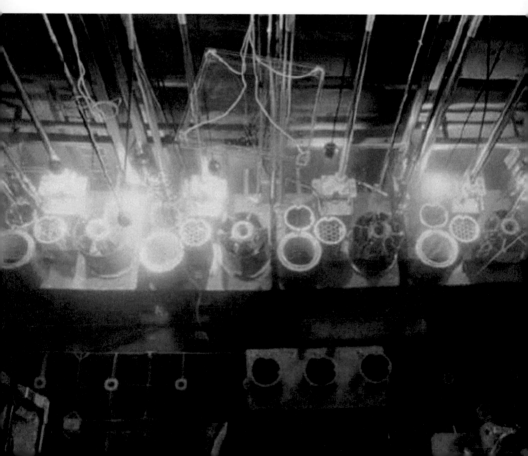

they had a program to enrich uranium for producing nuclear weapons, a direct violation of the 1994 agreement. Additionally, that same year, North Korea expelled United Nations nuclear inspectors who were carefully monitoring more than 8,000 plutonium rods. The inspectors were concerned because these rods could be developed into material for nuclear warfare.

In 2003 when the United States offered humanitarian aid to North Korea, if, in turn, North Korea would show good faith by decreasing their nuclear program, North Korea rejected the offer. In fact, the North Korean government strongly hinted that they were, at that time, reprocessing those rods for nuclear weapons and had reactivated their nuclear reactors. According to experts, the rods had the energy potential of twenty nuclear bombs. However, since inspectors had been hindered in their work and then expelled from the country, they were unable to determine if bombs had actually been made. Additionally, North Korea committed a threatening gesture by firing a missile into the Sea of Japan in March of that same year. Also in March, the government of North Korea said it would reject all demands to allow further nuclear inspections. In June, the United States insisted that not only did North Korea have to stop its nuclear weapons program completely, it also had to dismantle its program before talk of concessions or aid began. These conditions were set because previous efforts by the U.S. government to buy North Korean compliance had been unsuccessful. For instance, during the Clinton administration (1993–2000), the United States had tried such incentives as food, fuel, and committing to build North Korea two less dangerous nuclear plants, but North Korea continued churning out nuclear devices, despite its agreements not to do so.

North Korea responded by threatening to build a nuclear deterrent force that would be capable of neutralizing any attack and insisted that the United States end its hostile stance toward North Korea. Other verbal volleys were fired between the United States and North Korea, with North Korea, despite ongoing threats of its nuclear capabilities, claiming it has no uranium enrichment program and the United States insisting that it has. The United States also criticized Kim and North Korea for developing its nuclear program while allowing its people to go hungry.

Kim appears to delight in his role as a nuclear blackmailer. With his habit of threatening to renounce all previous agreements, which he appears to be ignoring anyway, the United States and its allies are well aware that North Korea is a serious problem. In fact, North Korea makes little effort to hide the fact that it has been doing nuclear-related business with Iran.

As Kim continued to posture and threaten, the United States and allied countries worked to figure out how to deal with this nuclear blackmail diplomatically, while avoiding a situation in which every country in proximity to North Korea felt the need

North Korean soldiers march near their country's border along China's Liaoning province, which is marked by a barbed wire fence constructed to keep North Korean refugees from crossing into the region.

to have its own nuclear deterrents. Such a scenario could lead to full-scale nuclear war in East Asia. Regarding diplomacy, China may be the key. Although Chinese relations with North Korea may not be as close as they once were, China still has some leverage over Kim. As of 2003 China was the North Korean's major source of food and fuel. Like the United States and other countries, China does not want Kim and North Korea to have nuclear armaments. In addition, North Korean refugees have overrun the Liaoning province in China, causing many problems in that region. It would be better for China if North Koreans remained in their own country and if the refugees in the economically depleted Liaoning province returned to North Korea.

Despite whoever acts as go-between, negotiations appear to have little effect on North Korean nuclear programs. North Korean officials stated that the country had performed its first nuclear test in October 2006 in the Hwaderi province, near Kilju City. China was given a twenty-minute warning of the impending test, and China told the United States, Japan, and South Korea. The closest North Korean ally, China, condemned the test and demanded that North Korea stop any further action that could make the situation worse.

The Chinese foreign ministry was outraged by this blatant display. They made their feelings known in a formal statement on their national website: "The DPRK (Democratic People's Republic of Korea) has ignored the widespread opposition of the international community and conducted a nuclear test brazenly on October 9."[17]

A little more than two years after the test, despite its earlier tough stance, the United States again promised North Korea food, fuel, and even the possibility of economic recognition in return for their good behavior. For its part, North Korea was expected to put a freeze on its plutonium facilities and allow nuclear inspectors admission to the sites. However, North Korea said that the deal the United States was offering was not enough. They also wanted back the $24 million in funds that had been frozen in the Banco Delta Asia of Macau, a measure the United States had taken when they suspected North Korea of counterfeiting American currency. This was an especially sensitive issue, because it is believed that if these funds are released, Kim will pocket the money and, as is his habit, violate his part of the agreement, likely conducting another bomb test, in a show of strength.

April 2007 brought another development in the talks, an announcement in the Chinese capital that, by December 31, North Korea would provide a complete list of its nuclear programs and allow an inspection team, led by the United States, to oversee the disabling of an experimental reactor, a nuclear fuel rod facility, and a reprocessing plant. However, by the end of 2007, nuclear talks were at another standstill.

According to a March 2008 article in the *Christian Science Monitor*, Kim was eager to talk about the issues of the December

Kim Jong Il's Sixty-fifth Birthday Bash

On February 16, 2007, a lavish production of military displays, huge precision dance troops, and flowery speeches marked the sixty-fifth birthday of Kim Jong Il. Korean television showed a huge flag of the Korean Workers' Party prominently displayed as a backdrop for a host of party dignitaries. In honor of the occasion, the state-controlled media issued this statement: "Your birth as a bright star of Mt. Paektu was the greatest event as it promised the happiness and prosperity of the Korean nation."

It appears the North Korean people may have to wait longer for this prosperity. In fact, analysts doubt that the citizens received the extra food ration that generally marks Kim's birthday. The country is experiencing chronic food shortages as well as economic sanctions.

Peter Walker, "Kim Jong Il Celebrates His 65th," *Guardian.co.uk*, February 16, 2007. www.guardian.co.uk/world/2007/feb/16/northkorea.

impasse. However, despite considerable proof to the contrary, he denies that the North Korean nuclear program is active. He also denies the charges that his country has been exporting nuclear aid to unstable areas such as Iran and Syria. Despite the lack of success of previous agreements with Kim and his officials, parties involved in the negotiations continue to hope for and work toward a resolution.

Kim's State of Health

If there is anything as uncertain in North Korea as the state of its nuclear agreements, it is the state of Kim Jong Il's health. First, according to sources, his eyesight is growing weak. He now relies on television, rather than newspapers, to keep up with world news, including reactions to his nuclear activities.

Other health-related issues are considerably more serious, such as the emergency heart bypass procedure he supposedly underwent in May 2007. Despite the cloak of secrecy that surrounds his personal life, sources say that a team of German doctors was flown into Pyongyang to perform the surgery. Allegedly, he also suffers from diabetes, high blood pressure, kidney and liver problems, and digestive problems. Reports state that Kim receives treatment, under extreme secrecy, for his other health problems in Beijing, China, because the North Korean health system is so inferior.

If these sources are to be believed, Kim's diabetes has progressed to the point that he cannot walk any distance without having to rest. Very short-winded, he must be accompanied by an assistant with a chair so he can sit and regain his breath. If this report is true, he could also be suffering from congestive heart failure.

As reclusive as he has been in recent years, his public appearances were even more curtailed in 2007 and 2008. He has only been seen in public a couple of dozen times since 2007, about half of the number of appearances of the previous year. The only positive report about his physical health is that he has stopped smoking and lost weight. He has even forbidden anyone to smoke

Kim Jong Il's public appearances declined significantly in the mid-2000s, causing observers to speculate that various health problems are taking their toll on the secretive North Korean leader.

in his presence. Wherever he goes, his surroundings immediately become no smoking areas. If his officials feel the need to smoke, they go outside. Accounts of his weight loss may not be an encouraging sign, however, as another report indicated Kim appeared physically emaciated, with dry skin and noticeable hair loss.

Some stories have circulated about Kim's mental condition as well. One intelligence source states that since about 2005 Kim has been suffering from symptoms that may be Alzheimer's Disease or senile dementia. Dementia is caused by damage to the cerebral nerve cells. This damage causes loss of memory and intelligence. Alzheimer's Disease is similar to senile dementia, except the earliest symptoms may appear as early as in one's forties or fifties. The first symptom is usually impaired memory, followed by difficulties with speech and thought. This pair of symptoms usually becomes apparent somewhere in the person's seventies. The condition finally progresses to complete helplessness.

Supposedly, his inner circle of aides is bypassing Kim on some policy decisions. Whereas Kim had always made decisions after personally approving reports submitted directly to him, his aides now handle some of these policy-making decisions, because they are concerned about his behavior and his mental state. His aides also worry about potential behavior problems when Kim goes on a tour. They are fearful of what he might do or say, and they are unable to control his sometimes strange behavior, which might include not recognizing some of his own key people or unprovoked angry outbursts.

As with many stories about Kim, it is difficult to verify this information. Official reports from North Korea indicate that Kim is fine and is taking care of business as usual. In fact, one report states that Kim's disappearance from public in 2007 is a political strategy to get international attention. The purpose of such a strategy, however, is unclear.

In October 2007 South Korean president Roh Moo Hyun traveled to Pyongyang to meet with Kim for the first North-South summit since the end of World War II, when the country was divided. The first evening of Roh's visit, Kim appeared pale and weak, but seemed recovered the next day. He told the press: "I have no reason to stay home. I'm not a patient."[18]

As to what could account for such a rapid turnaround in his physical appearance, one report out of East Asia in 2006 indicated that Kim has at least two exact doubles, men of a very similar body type to Kim, who had extensive plastic surgery and were taught to speak and behave like Kim at public events. It is said

Kim Jong Il speaks with South Korean president Roh Moo Hyun in Pyongyang at an October 2007 summit meeting between their nations, the first to be held since the end of World War II.

that their resemblance to Kim is so exact that it is difficult, even at close range, to tell whether the Kim presiding over an event is the real thing or one of his doubles. Supposedly, Kim uses these doubles when his health is poor, because as a dictator, it is not to his advantage to appear weak. They are also used when there is danger of an attack against Kim. Whether or not this is the explanation for Kim's drastic change during the summit is merely speculation.

Kim has supposedly responded to reports of his deteriorating health. Official North Korean sources say he called these accounts about his declining health the work of novelists. He insists that his health is still fine and that he is fully in charge of his country.

In 2008 at only sixty-seven years old, Kim was a bit young for the advanced effects of Alzheimer's or senile dementia, but his excessive lifestyle, including heavy partying and his consumption of large quantities of liquor and rich foods throughout his lifetime, could have caused the early onset of some potentially serious health conditions, such as diabetes and high blood pressure. His father, Kim Il Sung, died from a heart attack, and heart conditions run in families. Regardless of any reports supporting or denying health problems, these are conditions that may negatively affect the present and future condition of Kim's health.

Chances for Reunification

According to some analysts, North and South Korea have no desire to reunite. For such a reunification to take place, the North would have to abandon its nuclear program which, history has shown, is probably not on Kim's agenda. Kim's regime may also fear the thought of open trade, which goes against their principle of juche. Additionally, many South Koreans fear that unification might significantly lower their standard of living.

The United States and a number of other countries favor reunification. It could result in stronger east-west ties. It could also greatly reduce the burdens currently on the shoulders of U.S. peacekeepers, who are already spread thinly throughout the world.

Future Relations, Future Issues

Unsubstantiated reports concerning Kim's health have led to speculations about who will replace him, when the time comes. His brother-in-law, Chang Song Taek, husband of Kim's younger sister, Kim Kyung Hee, was one of his closest confidants and vice-director of the Organization and Guidance Department. Chang was described at one time as the number two man in North Korea. However, he apparently dropped from favored status in 2003 or 2004. He no longer lives with his wife, Kim's sister, but it is not known if this is the reason for his fall from favor.

Kim's eldest son, Kim Jong Nam, was at one time high on the list of potential successors. With a natural talent for languages and working with computers, he had some significant skills to bring to the table. However, he seriously damaged his opportunity due to his well-publicized attempt to sneak into Japan. He was arrested at the New Tokyo International Airport, now Narita International Airport, in Narita, Japan. After his arrest, he was deported to China. Apparently, he has not worked his way back into his father's good graces. As of 2006, he was living in exile in Macau, China. He moves from one five-star hotel to another, where he enjoys the nightlife and lives it up in and around the gambling capital of Asia.

Other possibilities include Kim's two sons by Ko Young Hee, Kim Jong Chul and Kim Jong Woong. Kim Jong Chul, Kim's eldest son by Ko Young Hee, was educated at the School of Berne in Switzerland under an assumed name. Students who knew him there referred to him as a "nice guy" and said he played on the basketball team. After school, he worked in the North Korean propaganda department and, in 2007, was named chief deputy of a leadership division of the Workers' Party. Because he is the elder of the two brothers, some people who have inside knowledge of North Korean government say he is being groomed for North Korea's highest post and that, although he has no military training himself, he nevertheless has the backing of the military. This support may have eroded, though, since his mother's death. Said to have been Kim Jong Il's favorite consort, she was often referred to as "esteemed mother" and "most loyal companion."

Kim Jong Nam, the high-living eldest son of Kim Jong Il, makes his way through a throng of reporters at an airport in Beijing, China, in 2007. A strained relationship between father and son complicates speculation on who will be the next leader of North Korea.

It is a possibility according to some people close to Kim that the dictator believes that Kim Jong Chul would not make a good successor because Kim thinks this particular son may be too soft and sensitive for the position.

Kim's youngest son by Ko Young Hee, Kim Jong Woong, is considered another strong contender. However, the issue of his age could get in the way of his succession. Only in his early twenties in 2008, analysts say he is far too young to lead the country, should Kim die. Of all potential successors, less is known about Kim Jong Woong. Many news agencies did not even know of his existence until about 2001. There are not even any known photographs of this young man. Like his older brother, he is thought to have been educated outside of North Korea and is also a basketball fan. Nicknamed "Morning Star King" by his late mother, those who know him say he looks, speaks, and acts much like his father, who apparently dotes on him.

Despite Kim Jong Woong's favored status with his father, Kim Jong Nam apparently still has some influence. Chung Hyung Geun, an official with an Asian conservative party, speculated about who would be the next leader of North Korea in an interview in 2006: "For now, (first son) Kim Jong Nam is said to be a favorite, but his carefree life got him into trouble with Kim Jong Il. However, since China supports Kim Jong Nam, this could touch off something like a 'war of princes.'"[19]

Regardless of who succeeds Kim, though, analysts say that a change in leadership could cause chaos in North Korea, which could lead to problems for other communist countries. China, for instance, fears that the fall of the North Korean government could lead to an even greater influx of North Koreans into China. They also fear that, if North and South Korea reunify, U.S. troops could some day be stationed on the border between China and Korea. Russia, too, is worried about a possible collapse of the communist government, the Workers' Party, in North Korea. Their concerns are much the same as those of the Chinese, an influx of North Koreans into Russia and the presence of U.S. troops on their borders.

Asia Times journalist, Sung Yoon Lee, predicts what the future could hold if Kim's regime collapses: "Should the regime collapse, providing North Korean refugees with basic necessities like food, water, medicine and shelter will be just one part of a large-scale crisis management project. The reconstruction of North Korea will be a monumental undertaking that will require the concerted effort of the international community."[20]

Should Kim Jong Il die anytime soon, his top military officers would probably take over. An extreme scenario for such a takeover would be tremendous loss of life in both North and South Korea as well as economic disaster for the entire Korean peninsula. At the very least, if the border between North and South Korea were thrown open, the North Koreans, isolated and brainwashed for decades, would likely suffer a severe culture shock. The most disastrous consideration, though, is the thought of nuclear weapons in a country in chaos.

However, if Kim's health holds out, he will still have time to groom his successor as well as to open the country to a more mainstream economy by putting more goods and property into the hands of average people, not just the privileged classes. Despite being the absolute ruler of North Korea, there may yet be time for Kim, if he is physically and mentally healthy enough, to make changes that would benefit his country and bring it into a more cooperative position with the rest of the world. Though his past behavior does not support such a spirit of cooperation, given the right circumstances, anything is possible.

Introduction: Controversy and Contradictions

1. Democratic People's Republic of Korea, "Kim Jong Il: Brief History," Korean Friendship Association, p. 5. www.Korea-dpr.com/pmenu.htm.
2. Discover the Networks, "Who is Kim Jong Il?" www.discoverthenetworks.org/individualProfile.asp?indid=2154.

Chapter 1: Privilege and Power

3. Quoted in Rachel A. Koestler-Grack, *Kim Il Sung and Kim Jong Il*. Philadelphia, PA: Chelsea House Publishers, 2004, p. 17.
4. Quoted in Michael J. Mazer, *Korea Economic Institute Academic Paper Series*, December 2006, Vol. 1, No.1, p. 2.
5. Quoted in Peter Maass, "The Last Emperor," *The New York Times Magazine*, October 19, 2003. http://www.petermaass.com/core.cfm?p=1&mag=111&magtype=1.

Chapter 2: Two Sides of Kim

6. Quoted in Bradley K. Martin, *Under the Loving Care of the Fatherly Leader*. New York: Thomas Dunne Books, 2004, p. 276.
7. Quoted in Martin, *Under the Loving Care of the Fatherly Leader*, p. 250.
8. Quoted in Martin, *Under the Loving Care of the Fatherly Leader*, p. 255.
9. Quoted in Martin, *Under the Loving Care of the Fatherly Leader*, p. 255.

Chapter 3: Grooming for Power

10. Quoted in Martin, *Under the Loving Care of the Fatherly Leader*, p. 245.
11. Quoted in Martin, *Under the Loving Care of the Fatherly Leader*, p. 333.
12. Quoted in Mike Thomson, "Kidnapped by North Korea,"

BBC News, March 5, 2003. http://news.bbc.co.uk/1/hi/world/
asia-pacific/2821221.stm.

Chapter 4: Dear Leader

13. Quoted in Don Oberdorfer, *Two Koreas*. New York: Basic
Books, 2001, p. 342.
14. Quoted in Jasper Becker, *Rogue Regime: Kim Jong Il and the
Looming Threat of North Korea*. New York: Oxford Press,
2005, p. 129.
15. Quoted in Becker, *Rogue Regime*, p. 131.
16. Quoted in Martin, *Under the Loving Care of the Fatherly Leader*,
p. 517.

Chapter 5: Kim's Legacy

17. Quoted in Jamie McIntyre, Barbara Starr, Sohn Jie-ae, and Elise
Labott, *North Korea Claims Nuclear Test*, CNN.Com, October
9, 2006. http://www.cnn.com/2006/WORLD/asiapcf/10/08/
korea.nuclear.test/.
18. Quoted in Jonathan Watts, "I'm Not Suffering Health
Problems, Says Kim Jong Il," Guardian.com.uk, October 3,
2007. http://www.guardian.co.uk/world/2007/oct/03/north-
korea2.
19. Quoted in Bill Powell, "A World Without Kim," Time.
com, September 11, 2008. www.time.com/time/magazine/
article/0,9171,1840408,00.html.
20. Quoted in Lee Seung Woo, "Kim Jong Il in Bad Health, Serious
Walking Problem," *Yonhap News*, September 6, 2006. http://
www.freerepublic.com/focus/f-news/1696439/posts.

1910–1945

The Korean peninsula is annexed and ruled by Japan.

1942

Kim Jong Il is born to Kim Il Sung and Kim Jong Suk.

1945

Japan surrenders to Allied forces. Japanese forces on the Korean peninsula north of the thirty-eighth parallel surrender to the Soviet Union; forces south of the thirty-eighth parallel surrender to the United States.

Kim Jong Il's family returns to Korea, their home country.

1947

Kim Jong Il's younger brother, Kim Pyong Il, drowns.

1949

Kim Jong Il's mother dies in childbirth.

1950

The Korean Conflict begins.

Kim Jong Il and his younger sister, Kim Kyong Hee, are sent to China for their safety during the Korean conflict.

1953

The Korean conflict ends, and Kim Jong Il and his sister return to Pyongyang, the capital city of North Korea.

1964

Kim Jong Il graduates from Kim Il Sung University.

1966

Kim marries his first wife, Hong Il Chon.

1971

Kim and Hong Il Chon divorce.

1973

Kim marries Kim Yong Suk

1975

North Korea produces its first plutonium.

1978

Kim Jong Il plans and has carried out the kidnapping of popular South Korean actress, Choi Eun Hee, and her ex husband, director, Shin Sang Ok.

1983

Seventeen members of a South Korean delegation visiting Burma are killed by a bomb said to have been planted by North Korean agents.

1985

North Korea signs the International Nuclear Nonproliferation Treaty.

1987

North Korea is held responsible for a bomb that explodes on a Korean Airlines jet, killing all 155 passengers.

1993

North Korea withdraws from the International Nuclear Nonproliferation Treaty.

1994

The death of Kim Il Sung, Kim Jong Il's father, is announced. North Korea signs the Agreed Framework, in which the country agrees to halt the development of nuclear weapons in return for help in building civilian nuclear reactors and also for receiving temporary oil supplies.

1995

Massive floods hit North Korea, causing loss of life, destruction of farmlands, and resultant food shortages.

1997

Kim Jong Il is named General Secretary of the Korean Workers' Party.

1998

North Korea announces that, not only will it continue to build nuclear missiles, it will export them as well.
Food shortages made even more critical by severe drought.

2001

Kim Jong Il's eldest son, Kim Jong Nam, is arrested in Japan, traveling on a counterfeit passport, and is deported to China.

2003

North Korea's news agency declares nuclear reactors are reactivated.
North Korea fires a missile into the Sea of Japan.
North Korea refuses international demands to allow nuclear inspectors in the country.

2004

Pakistani scientist, A. Q. Khanh, admits passing uranium enrichment technology to North Korea, Libya, and Iran.

2006

North Korea performs first nuclear test.

2007

North Korea indicates its willingness to provide a list of all its nuclear programs, but talks stall at year-end.

2008

Kim again agrees to return North Korea to the bargaining table, but denies that the North Korean nuclear program is presently active.

For More Information

Books

Tim Beal, *North Korea: The Struggle Against American Power*. Ann Arbor, MI: Pluto Press, 2005. For somewhat more advanced readers, this volume is divided into two parts. The first section touches on the early history of Korea, the Korean Conflict, and the beginning and the fall of the Agreed Framework. Part two includes the North Korean human rights record, illegal drug activity, and possible options for the future. Written from a variety of perspectives, not necessarily flattering to the United States.

William Dudley, ed., *North and South Korea*. Detroit, MI: Greenhaven Press, 2003. This volume is a collection of articles expressing opposing viewpoints about North and South Korea, North Korea's nuclear programs, relationship issues between the two countries, and speculations about the future of North Korea's nuclear programs.

Scott Ingram, *Kim Il Sung*. Farmington Hills, MI: Blackbirch Press, 2004. Describes the political times in which Kim Il Sung, father of Kim Jong Il, was born and raised during the Japanese occupation of the Korean peninsula. It includes what many to believe to be his actual birth name, Kim Song Ju, his family background, and the ways the Japanese occupation of his country and the accompanying cruelties and atrocities may have influenced the kind of person he became.

Rachel A. Koestler-Grack, *Kim Il Sun and Kim Jong Il*. Philadelphia, PA: Chelsea House, 2004. This book carries the reader through the life of Kim Il Sung and the political climate of the country during Japanese occupation, the liberation, and Kim's rise to power. The book then transitions to Kim Jong Il's childhood, his being named his father's sole successor, his own rise toward leadership, the death of his father, and the ongoing North Korean nuclear conflicts.

Debra Miller, ed., *North Korea*. Detroit, MI: Greenhaven Press, 2004. This book contains a collection of articles about North Korea, including its early history, the division of Korea, North Korean nuclear weapons and human rights abuses, and its isolationism and economic woes.

Suk Hi Kim, *North Korea at a Crossroads*. Jefferson, NC: McFarland and Company, Inc., 2003. This book is a brief, objective interpretation of the history of Korea, the split between the North and the South, the North Korean principle of self reliance, and its economy. It concludes with a chapter citing reasons why other countries should reconcile with and help North Korea.

Web Sites

Asia Times Online (www.atimes.com/) This is an online news publication featuring current articles relevant to Asian countries.

The Cook Energy Center (www.cookinfo.com/nuclearwebs.htm) This site provides a table of links to student-based resources pertaining to nuclear organizations, national laboratories, and government agencies.

Kim Jong Il News (http://kim-jong-il-news.newslib.com/) This site provides links to articles written about Kim Jong Il in recent months.

Korea.net: Gateway to Korea (www.korea.net) This website is about South Korea. It provides an interesting contrast to the official site of North Korea. It includes tourism, business, and even a section about the religions of South Korea.

The Official Webpage of the Democratic People's Republic of Korea (DPRK) (www.korea-dpr.com/) This is the official website of the controlling political party of North Korea. In entering this site, it is important to bear in mind that all information included in this site is under the jurisdiction of the government and the party. This site includes information pertaining to business, tourism, and culture as well as highly idealized biographies of Kim Il Sung and Kim Jong Il.

Korean Conflict, 24–25
Korean resistance movement,
14–15, *15*
See also Guerilla fighters;
Japanese occupation
Korean Workers Party. *See*
North Korean Workers'
Party

Lee Young Guk, 65

March First movement, 17
Missiles. *See* Nuclear
Nonproliferation Treaty
(NPT); Nuclear research and
development; Scud missiles
Motion pictures. *See* Movies
Mount Paektu, 19, 20
Movies
direct involvement, 39–40
early interest, 33
industry role, 40
Kim Jong Il's, 38, 39, 53
moviemaking representa-
tion, *36–37*
obsession with, 53–56

Natural disasters, 65, 66
Neighboring countries, 74, 75
North Korea
allies, 51
bankruptcy, 67
borders, 22, 23, 78
capital, 32
economic hardships, 52,
65–67
infant mortality rate, 67
isolation, 51, 67
living standards, 67
origins, 22

political philosophy and
atmosphere, 47–48, 49,
50, 51–52
propaganda, 51
surveillance of citizens, 48,
62
trade agreements, 65
North Korean Workers' Party,
33, 34, 38, 40, 50, 61
Nuclear Nonproliferation
Treaty (NPT), 70, 71, 72
Nuclear research and
development
as blackmail, 68, 74, 78
history, 12–13, 69–74
international incidents, 72
international sanctions, 68
ongoing negotiations, 80–81
treaty violations, 75, 76–77,
79

Pakistan, 13
The Path to Awakening (movie),
38
People's Democratic Republic
of North Korea. *See* North
Korea
Personality cult, 46, 47–48,
49, *49*, 51
Plutonium, 70, 71
Privacy. *See* Surveillance
Pyongyang, North Korea, 32,
32, 34

Republic of Korea. *See* South
Korea
Rockets, 56, 73
Roh Moo Hyun, 84
Russia. *See* Soviet Union

Cover: Getty Images
AFP/Getty Images, 70, 82
AP Images, 11, 18, 49, 50, 66, 69, 76, 78, 84, 87
© Adrian Bradshaw/epa/Corbis, 46
Choongang Monthly Magazine/Newsmakers/Getty Images, 57
© Corbis Sygma, 21, 26, 61
© epa/Corbis, 73
Gale, Cengage Learning, 23
© Handout/Reuters/Corbis, 30
Kyodo/Landov, 34
© Alain Nogues/Corbis, 36–37, 44, 63
Popperfoto/Getty Images, 15
Karl Schumacher/Time Life Pictures/Getty Images, 54
Topical Press Agency/Hulton Archive/Getty Images, 16
Wang Tae-Suk-Pool/Getty Images, 32

A retired middle school teacher, Sheila Wyborny and her husband, a consulting engineer, live in an airport community near Houston, Texas. Since her retirement, she has written over two dozen nonfiction books for elementary and secondary students.